THE
ADOPTION
ADVISER

Joan McNamara

An Information House Book

HAWTHORN BOOKS, INC.
Publishers/NEW YORK

THE ADOPTION ADVISER

Library of Congress Catalog Card Number: 74-18693
ISBN: 0-8015-0068-0
1 2 3 4 5 6 7 8 9 10

THE
ADOPTION
ADVISER

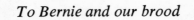

To Bernie and our brood

Contents

Contents

Preface

This book grew out of a handbook idea for the Citizens Coalition for Children. Like so many undertakings in adoption, it expanded and grew into something more.

When my husband and I first looked into adoption, it was with the notion of expanding our family while providing a home to a child who had none. We did not imagine then the ways in which our family would grow—in size, in outlook, and in spirit. Our horizons widened with new cultures, new perspectives, and new personalities to cope with. Discovering in each other what Quakers call the "inner light," we have all been touched by what each has brought to this union.

Along the way we became more deeply involved in many different aspects of adoption, joining others in helping waiting children and families to find each other. Sometimes the information gathered about adoption from various sources was confusing, contradictory, or out of date. At other times an unexpected encounter would bring insights. As information and insights accumulated, its value to other parents in other areas of the country, asking the same questions we had asked, was apparent. And so started the task of assembling and organizing the bits and pieces into a simple, cohesive form.

Preface

The Adoption Adviser is a beginning, to help you with the very first steps in adoption and direct you to other resources that can take you still further: agencies, books, exchanges, special programs, and other parents. If this book has been helpful, I hope that your particular adoption experience will expand your lives as much as ours have.

Acknowledgments

The author wishes to thank:

The late Janet Feldman, caseworker and friend;

Dr. Wayne McKinney of Tom Dooley Memorial Hospital, Laos, and godfather to so many children;

Bernard H. McNamara, M.S.W., C.S.W., for his professional and personal guidance;

And to the many families across the country who have shared, especially to AFW and OURS, and to Jessie Strauss in particular.

Information House wishes to thank Peggy Bedoya, Joyce Shue, Anne Columbia, Irit Spierer, Charles Heckelmann, and Ron Shafer.

THE
ADOPTION
ADVISER

Introduction

Adoption of children is an ever changing tradition. In ancient Rome, the purpose of adoption was to provide elder men with sons to carry on the family name. By the mid-1920s in the United States, the goal was to find children for childless couples. Today the emphasis is on what is best for the adopted child.

Meanwhile, adoption has become an increasingly acceptable method for starting or expanding a family. Once largely limited to upper-middle-income white couples, adoption today is available to a broader range of people than ever before. Federal agencies estimate there are 2.5 million adopted children in the United States, about 2 percent of the child population. In 1973 nearly 90,000 children were adopted, not including an almost equal number of adoptions by relatives.

In past years, most nonrelative adoptions involved infants —mainly white infants—adopted by infertile or childless couples of similar national or racial backgrounds. But gradual changes have taken place in adoptions. For one thing, due to increasing use of the pill and abortions, fewer infants (of any racial background) are available for adoption. As a result,

1

adoption experts say the number of adoptions is temporarily declining.

At the same time, more families of diverse background are applying to adopt. Increasingly, more applicants are nonwhite couples, couples who may already have children, single people, and couples with average or below-average incomes. Such people, for the most part, previously were excluded from the adoption picture either because of actual adoption agency policies or due to the public concept of adoption. These families, as well as more and more childless couples, are reaching out to adopt children who usually were bypassed before: older children, children with medical or psychological problems, children of various racial and national backgrounds.

It wasn't always that way. In ancient civilizations of Greece, Rome, India, and the Far East—as well as more primitive cultures—the main purpose of adoption was to continue male patterns of inheritance, not to aid homeless children. The emphasis on inheritance, which meant that only healthy young boys were likely to be adopted, continued into the nineteenth century. At that time, other orphaned or abandoned children, who had no relatives or others to informally claim them, were sent to poorhouses or orphanages.

By the middle of the nineteenth century, public opinion forced reforms in laws and practices governing homeless children in the United States. Massachusetts was the first state to develop safeguards for indigent children without homes, and it permitted legal adoptions in 1851. Social and charitable organizations devoted to the care and protection of homeless children sprang up in many places. Foster care was begun. By the end of the century, many states required protection of prospective adoptive children through investigations of potential adoptive homes.

By 1927 all states had adoption laws. In a move to avoid previous abuses, the newly recognized profession of social work established adoption requirements designed to protect the welfare of adopted children. Since social work was predominately a white, middle-class profession, so were the standards used to judge the acceptability of adoptive parents. Generally, only childless couples were accepted by agencies. And they could only adopt children who were matched by the social workers to the family's genetic, physical, and intellectual makeup. Adopted babies were to be as close as possible to the child that the adoptive couple could not bear.

As more couples began to apply, many social agencies became more selective, demanding that applicants meet rigid qualifications of age, health, infertility, religion, and finances. Prospective parents increasingly became discouraged from approaching adoption agencies because of high standards and high costs. Many began to circumvent established avenues by venturing into "gray" and "black" markets for babies; that is, they adopted children directly through private sources, such as doctors or lawyers, rather than through recognized agencies, sometimes illegally in the case of "black market" adoptions. This economic and social pressure made it especially difficult for low-income minority couples to adopt children.

Independent adoptions, or those without the aid or protection of licensed agencies, continued to increase until after World War II. Finally, many agencies were forced to reevaluate their practices as the result of an unexpected decrease in applications. Adoption officials realized that, by trying to protect children, many agencies actually had set up barriers to their adoption. They had created such arbitrary standards for prospective parents that children were losing opportunities for homes.

The agencies began to become more flexible and realistic in their approach to prospective parents. Meanwhile, such prestigious groups as the Child Welfare League of America led the way in establishing that the prime objective of adoption is to place children in homes that best serve *their* well-being, not simply to locate children for families. For the first time, agencies began to actively and aggressively recruit parents for so-called "hard-to-adopt" children in their care. By the 1960s the emphasis had shifted from finding the perfect baby for the perfect family to locating a family with the desire and ability to raise an adopted child—a child who could be of any age, of any racial background, with any medical condition.

Just when agencies were becoming more flexible and when prospective parents were responding by approaching adoption in greater numbers, the children traditionally considered "most adoptable" became less available. The number of illegitimate infants began to decrease dramatically as more women used contraceptives or got abortions. "Blue-ribbon babies," primarily white, healthy infants, no longer were given up for adoption in such large numbers as before because of a changing moral climate in which more single women kept their out-of-wedlock children.

Those trends are continuing. With fewer infants up for adoption, many adoptive parents are turning to children who in previous years would have been left in foster care or institutions until adolescence or adulthood—children beyond infancy, children with medical problems, and children from other countries. There are increasing adoptions of American Indian, black, mixed-race, and other minority group children. Previously such children generally remained in foster care or institutions because families of the same background could not meet strict agency standards or were discouraged by those standards.

Much of the pioneer work has been completed in adoption. With new information now available on the changes and experimental trends of the past few years, more and more people of all races and backgrounds can venture into adoption on a secure basis—to find joy in raising a child brought into their families through a means they once might not even have considered.

Today prospective adoptive parents may include couples

without children, couples with children, couples where the wife intends to continue working, single people, older couples who may have particular patience in dealing with school age children, apartment dwellers with limited space, families who lack big bank accounts and may need financial assistance in order to adopt, families who can make room for one more, and families who will need special help for the emotional, physical, or financial problems of a handicapped child.

The most important requirement in the adoption process is the ability to love an adopted child and to help that child grow into responsible adulthood.

1

The Decision to Adopt

You are about to make one of the most important decisions of your life. Not just the decision to adopt or not to adopt, although that surely is an important question. But first you must decide if you truly want to take the plunge into parenthood and if you are willing to devote a large chunk of your life, or lives, to a growing human being who will demand inordinate amounts of your time, your energies, and your love.

So the first question you should ask yourself is, "Why do I want children at all, adopted or otherwise?"

The question may seem silly; you would not be thinking about adoption if you did not want children. But your reasons for wanting them can make the difference between a child being a blessing and a challenge or an annoyance and a burden.

For example, some people assume that children are automatic necessities in married life. For some couples, not having children in the house would be like not having indoor plumbing. Unthinkable and embarrassing. They want children because it is expected of them, when in fact they may not really be interested in children, or they may not have the dispositions necessary to raise a family.

Other people may want children because they have an overly romantic view of what it is like to have kids of their own. Your own notions, if you are not around children much, could be in for severe testing when you are put in constant contact with the reality of little ones (and, later, bigger ones). Don't think only in terms of the potential satisfaction of helping children grow into worthwhile adults; consider also those day-to-day moments of messy diapers and runny noses.

Still other people may want a child to fill an empty life, to keep a marriage together, or to give them something to do in the evening before the 9 o'clock movie comes on TV. In short, merely wanting children is not enough, or shouldn't be.

In considering why you want children, you really are asking if your reasons are valid ones and if you want children for themselves or mainly for your own satisfaction. You no doubt have your own reasons, good ones, for wanting children. There are a couple of basic good reasons that you especially should keep in mind.

For one, do you enjoy children, including the responsibilities and obligations they bring? This means you understand what is involved in raising children and still are willing to go ahead with this glorious insanity.

Second, can you give something of value to a child? Not in a material sense but in terms of guidance and understanding, discipline and affection, and the capacity to deal with problems as they arise. Parenthood takes maturity and strength. To paraphrase a famous presidential speech, you should ask not what a child can do for you but what you can do for a child.

Fortunately, the decision to start a family is an increasingly serious one today for many people. And the number of children in a family is more likely to be a matter of choice instead of just biology. This is true both for couples who decide to have many children and for those who decide one or two are plenty. Couples who decide not to have any children no longer are as likely to be scorned as in the past and, indeed, are lauded by those worried about overpopulation.

Adoption is an integral part of the trend toward family planning. Couples who wish to have more than the socially ordained two children per family often are admonished by doctors, friends, and relatives to consider adoption as an expansion route. Adoption has become a socially acceptable alternative for couples who, for reasons of infertility, can't have children biologically. Childless couples who can have children but wish to start a family by adopting also are part of today's adoption picture. And so, too, are single people.

If you are considering adoption, a close look at why you want children cannot be avoided. You will be asked to deeply examine your feelings and motivations. It may be the first time you have ever had to do so. As a result, an adoption agency homestudy can be a slightly unsettling experience.

That is why it is important to consider now why you want children, to determine if your reasons seem sound. And, if they do not, to consider what you can do to change your attitudes or to seek help to change them.

First, let us look at reasons *not* to have children. While the following motivations may contribute to your views of parenthood, none should be the exclusive reason for wanting a child.

Status. Are there business or social expectations, or pressures from friends and relatives to have children? Children still are often thought of as standard equipment for happily married couples. Many companies favor "family men" (although they may frown on "family women" in the same jobs). For couples married longer than a year without having children, parental pressure to produce grandchildren is common. Despite inroads made by such groups as the National Organization for Non-Parents (NON), married people without children still are considered odd in many social sets.

Such pressures should be resisted. It is unfair for you to be forced to raise children because of other people's expectations.

It is unfair not only to you but especially to the child raised in a family where he or she was not really wanted because of himself but because he was expected to be there.

Traditions. Do you want a child to carry on your business, your profession, or your interests? Or do you just want a boy to carry on your family name? If so, think carefully about the impact on you, and especially on your child, if he or she cannot cooperate with your plans or doesn't share your interests. As for having a son to preserve the family name—if he thought that was your only interest, you might in fact end up having a son in name only.

All parents have dreams and aspirations for their children. But each child is an individual of undetermined potential. Parents have to learn to keep their own plans in perspective. They must be able to guide, without living through their children's lives. A child cannot be merely a vehicle to fulfill family or individual traditions.

Boredom. Are you bored with your life? Do you need to occupy time or to give affection? It may be that you are not fulfilled without being able to raise a child. Then again, it may be that you simply need a change of scene, a pet, or an opportunity to meet new people. Perhaps your desire to busy yourself or to touch others would be best accomplished by doing volunteer work in schools or hospitals where you can satisfy your needs without the long-term obligation that raising children requires.

A child is not a cure for boredom. In fact, feminists say children may perpetuate feelings of frustration and inadequacy for some women. For some mothers, nothing is more stultifying than being "trapped" in the home with preschool children, with little opportunity for adult conversation or interests during the day. On the other hand, increasing numbers of women are avoiding the "baby trap" by returning to work, by arranging day care or cooperative babysitting, and by sharing interests with other mothers in similar situations.

The point is to make sure you are not confusing some other

need with the desire to have children. Adoption agencies are particularly strict about this with single parents. They want to be sure that single people are not lonely people who are adopting mainly because they cannot have dogs in their apartments or because they have not yet found mates.

Most agencies prefer adoptive parents—singles or couples —who are content with themselves and their lives, and who therefore have a positive relationship to offer a child. Unhappy people usually do not make the best parents, adoptive or biological.

Problems. Do you have personal conflicts you feel would improve if only you had a child? Do you think that raising children would compensate for past mistakes in your life? Do you want a child to replace a son or daughter who died? Do you want children to save your marriage?

If you want to correct errors made in the past, talk to a psychiatrist. If you want to prove that you can accomplish something, try writing a book. But don't make a child a project to satisfy unmet needs. Few problems are eased by adding a child to your life, and most are intensified. Children will not treat an emotional problem, compensate for the loss of a loved one, or strengthen an unstable marriage.

Nearly everybody has some problems. Adoption workers are mainly interested in how you cope with them. Your maturity in dealing with problems can be more important than the difficulties themselves. But adoption workers will not consider the need to solve a problem as a valid reason to have a child.

Once you have determined that you want children for positive reasons, you can consider adoption. That raises a whole new group of questions. Each approach to adoption is different, and only you, with your worker, can evaluate your individual case. But there are some basic questions to ask yourself, including the most basic of all: Can I accept a child who was not born of me or my spouse?

10

If you are married, you probably did not select your mate because he or she has brown eyes and so do you. And you did not decide to marry because you both are color-blind or share some other hereditary trait. You probably saw something of value in each other, and you committed yourselves to sharing your lives because of a bond of love that took time to grow and develop. The same is true of adoption. There is the commitment of two people to a third, to a child, because of a potential for a growing bond of love that soon will be returned.

Certainly physical appearances and other external factors influence how we feel about others, at least initially. But if you have the ability to love another person who is different from yourself, you have the ability to love an adopted child.

•   Do I consider adoption a normal and positive way to have a child become part of my family?

This question is especially important for infertile couples who may be turning to adoption after fruitless attempts to produce children biologically. Adoption cannot be a "second-best" proposition if you and your child are to have a healthy relationship. Similarly, all adoptive parents should beware of the "rescuer–poor unfortunate" syndrome, which is the idea that by adoption you are "saving" a child from growing up in some dreary institution. A child should not have to grow up feeling grateful or somehow inferior.

If you have biological children, or if there is a possibility that you may be able to produce children later, you should especially consider whether you can accept an adopted child as your own. Adoption workers for many years used the "rowboat story" to gauge people's feelings toward adopted versus biological children. It went like this:

If you were in a rowboat with your two children, one adopted and the other born to you, and the boat tipped over, which would you save first? The question is ridiculous. But it once was asked in great seriousness to determine if an adopted child placed with a family might be relegated to a secondary

11

place in the family structure. Most applicants, by the way, gave such sensible and pragmatic answers as "the child who couldn't swim" or "the closest one."

Fortunately, the rowboat story has gone the way of the *Titanic*. But you should realistically evaluate your own feelings toward adoption in cases where there also is, or may be, a biological child in the family. If an adopted child would be replaced by a long-awaited "bio" child, then both children would be put into an unfair and detrimental situation.

On the other hand, adoption in any family should not be so exalted that the adopted child gets a distorted view of his own importance. This is particularly true in families where there also is a biological child, who might be the one to feel inferior —"Mom and dad *chose* our adopted baby. They had to take what they got with me."

Adoption or childbirth, it is all part of the same normal process of establishing a family that grows together through love, hard work, and cooperation. With a few spats mixed in.

• Can I deal with information about my child's past, or with the complete lack of information?

Children are released for adoption for many reasons. They may be illegitimate. They may have been removed from abusive or neglectful parents. They may have been abandoned by parents who did not have the resources to properly take care of them, especially if the child has medical problems. They may have been orphaned because of war.

You probably have different reactions to each reason, colored by your experiences and beliefs. As an adoptive parent, you will in many cases receive rather detailed information about your child's biological parents, especially the mother. Your reactions could affect the way you respond to your adopted child. For example, if you strongly believe that all unwed mothers are immoral, your attitude could be com-

12

municated to your child, perhaps unconsciously, with resulting damage to the child's self-image.

For some adopted children, there is little or no information about parents, medical history, or background. This means it will be difficult or impossible to eventually tell a child much about his biological parents or his life before joining your family. It also means there are no prenatal health records, no shot records, and no clues to possible hereditary conditions.

Like all children, an adopted child eventually will want to know, "Where did I come from?" It is up to the adoptive parent to help the child develop positive feelings about adoption, about his past, and about himself. Possible questions from prying relatives, curious friends, and playmates in the neighborhood make it especially important that an adopted child be able to get straightforward answers from the adoptive parents.

• For couples only, do each of you truly want to adopt children?

Just as marriage is a partnership, so too is raising a child. If one of you is going along with adoption plans because of the desires of the other, you may not be able to adequately accept an adopted child. Such a child needs the love and support of both marriage partners as well as the security of feeling wanted by each partner. A child is not a gift you give your spouse or an amusement you allow in your house because it pleases your wife or husband. You both should be committed to the idea of raising children and to the concept of obtaining them through adoption.

If one of you is infertile, make sure you are not pondering adoption to placate your spouse's possible feelings of inadequacy for not being able to help produce a baby. If you are a childless couple by choice, make sure both of you are ready to revamp your adult-oriented lifestyle by adopting a child. If you already have children, be certain you are not adopting when only one of you feels the need for more.

13

If you candidly admit you are not enthusiastic about adopting children, try to approach the subject with an open mind; learn more before making a final decision. Some people who initially are less interested in adoption than their spouses eventually turn out to be among the most devoted parents of all.

A Little Help from Your Friends

As you try to make up your mind about adoption, you may find it helpful to share your thoughts with other people. They may be professionals, social service volunteers, relatives, or just friends who can lend a sympathetic ear over a cup of coffee; each may offer insights and advice you each might not have considered. Just remember that even the best of friends and other advisers may be fountains of misinformation on the subject of adoption if they haven't had much experience with this particular method of planned parenthood.

One place you can turn to in many communities is an adoptive parents group. By talking to other couples (or singles) who have adopted, and by meeting with their children, you may get a better idea of how adoption would meet your needs. They also can give you the lowdown on what to expect from local adoption agencies and the courts. The groups may have preadoptive meetings in which you can take part. Or they may be able to direct you to professional counselors with experience in dealing with adoptions.

A listing of adoptive parents groups is included in the directory of this book. Check with several groups near you. Some groups concentrate on problems of childless couples who adopt, others focus on interracial or international adoptions, and still others may have a diverse membership reflecting many interests. If you find a group with activities that interest you, ask to be put on a mailing list. Most groups publish a monthly newsletter. You usually can receive it without being a member of the group, although there usually is a fee to cover postage.

With some adoptions, you may want or need even more specialized help, for example, if you want to adopt a child with a physical or mental handicap. One centralized contact for such help is AASK—Aid to the Adoption of Special Kids. AASK (its address is listed in the directory of this book) can help you find preadoption guidance on the local level and can direct you to local groups that can fill more concrete post-adoption needs. For instance, a Rotary Club may be able to provide a wheelchair, the parent-teacher association a tutor, or a state agency some financial support.

After you have considered basic questions about adoption, you are ready to look at some specifics involving your own situation. Each case is different, but there are certain "who adopts" categories that can be discussed. They are:

The Infertile Couple

If you cannot have children biologically, one of the first questions an adoption agency will ask you is, "Are you able to accept your infertility?"

This is for two reasons:

First, if you view your inability to produce children as a "failure" on your part or on the part of your spouse, or as some shameful inadequacy, then the child you adopt may become a symbol of this "failure." Rather than being a source of joy, the child may be a reminder to one or both of you that "There is something wrong with me."

Second, some infertile couples are misled by stories about childless couples who adopt and soon afterward the wives become pregnant. If you hope that adoption will stimulate conception, you are not only medically off-base but you are using a child as a means to attain another purpose. This is when adoption becomes a matter of "second best." You still won't have what you really want—a biological child—and you may resent the substitute. No child should grow up being considered second best. Every child deserves a family that loves her for herself because of the special person she is.

Of course, adoption may not have been considered until you discovered you could not have children biologically. But once you have accepted your infertility, adoption can be a positive, first choice for having the children you want. If you can separate the desire to conceive children from the desire to raise children, adoption becomes a logical alternative. You might want to talk to some adoptive parents; many of those who couldn't produce children likely will tell you their infertility was a blessing in disguise because otherwise they might never have adopted the kids they now love as their own.

If you or your spouse has an infertility problem, you may need help to deal with it even before you reach the stage of discussion about adoption. Some people are not very disturbed by their inability to biologically produce a child, and they glide quite easily into the decision to adopt. But for many wives, it may be a blow to discover they will not be able to experience what often is portrayed as the ultimate experience for a woman—pregnancy and childbirth. Many men wrongly interpret their own infertility as a lack of masculinity.

So it may take time and some emotional anguish to accept the fact that the possibility of bearing a child is so remote that it is time to stop trying. Infertility can be a complex, difficult thing to deal with because it can raise doubts about sexuality, self-worth, and marital relationships. Having someone to talk to about your feelings may help you put them, and your self-esteem, in the proper perspective. You might want to talk to a marriage counselor or a clergyman, or seek psychological advice. Or, as suggested earlier, you might seek out members of a local adoptive parents group who may have gone through a similar experience.

Women can get personal and informal guidance in many communities from a group called RESOLVE (a central address is listed in the appendix). At a RESOLVE group, women discuss problems involved not only with infertility but with such issue as miscarriage, stillbirth, and infant death with other women who have had similar experiences. In discussing infertility, RESOLVE members also may explore lifestyle alternatives of childlessness and adoption. Members say the basic need of many infertile couples is to acknowledge and deal with their true feelings about their infertility and about adoption.

If you decide adoption is a positive alternative for having children, you may find your infertility is an advantage. Many adoption agencies try to reserve the dwindling number of infants available for adoption for couples who cannot have babies otherwise. At some agencies, such adoptive couples also may get some priority for a second child on the theory that it is best for the adopted first child to have a brother or sister rather than to grow up as an only child.

The Childless Couple

If you are childless by choice, you may run into old prejudices when you decide to adopt. Many people assume that, if you had the choice (and the physical ability), you would have "your own" children. This attitude in part is a carryover from the old idea that adopted children are a second choice in families. And despite inroads made by the zero population growth groups, many still look with suspicion on the couple who decides to adopt rather than add to a people-jammed planet.

You will face still more obstacles at adoption agencies. The most basic one is that, with fewer children available for adoption these days, agencies may hesitate to place babies with couples who could have children on their own. You will have to explain and re-explain your reasons for adopting, especially

17

if you have not attempted to have children. Probably the most acceptable reasons are medical, such as the desire not to pass on hereditary conditions or the possibility that childbirth could endanger the wife's life.

If your motives for adopting are humanitarian, you should examine them closely. Maybe you were moved by a television show that presented appealing yet hard-to-place children in need of adoptive homes. Or perhaps you read news stories about starving and homeless orphans in distant countries. Certainly such children are worthy of your consideration if you do adopt. But if your prime motive is a sense of duty or obligation toward poor unfortunate children, then you and they would be better off if you donated time, money, or materials to efforts to help such children.

To rescue a child from an overcrowded orphanage or a war-torn country makes marvelous magazine stories, but it is not the stuff everyday living is made of. Pity is a terrible basis for a relationship. Unless you are prepared to love a child because of himself, and not because of his exotically deprived past, do not consider adopting an underprivileged child.

If you are childless intentionally (unless there is a medical reason), adoption agencies probably also will ask both of you to think twice about giving up your chosen lifestyle. Right now you are pretty much free to do what you want when you want to do it. With a child in the house, you won't be able to duck out to the movies on a whim. Those quiet evenings at home will be shattered by the screaming of little lungs. And the extra money that may now go to dinner and show may have to be used for cribs or blue jeans (depending on the age of the adoptee). As a result, your adoption worker will want to know about your relationship as a couple, so do your homework ahead of time.

If you plan to have biological children later, you will be asked how you will deal with the relationship between your adopted children and your "bio" children. Some agencies will even counsel you to come back after you have had children biologically. If you are determined you really prefer to adopt for solid reasons, you are going to have to be firm in your convictions and keep trying even if rebuffed.

The Couple with Children

If you already have started a family, you will not be viewed with quite as much suspicion as the couple who decides to adopt first. However, you will generally have to consider the "hard-to-place" or older child rather than the "blue-ribbon" infant. At a time when demand is high and adoptable infants are in short supply, you have already had your chance, so to speak, to take care of a baby.

You may be joining the ranks of those who have decided to expand their families without adding to the population explosion by bringing another child into the world. Or perhaps you simply have not been able to conceive another child for some time and are turning to a more certain route. That is fine as far as it goes, but you should beware of certain pitfalls:

• Are you out to "save" an unfortunate child from a life of misery by taking her into your happy home? Children are better off without such sentiments, however idealistic or noble. If an adopted child is going to be spoiled because "she never had anything before," you will end up with a child who is both a brat and unhappy. Your other children will resent such a "special" child unless she learns to act like the rest of the family and you begin to treat her that way.

On the other hand, if you feel that a child in need also could fulfill your desire to add to your family, then adoption of such a child may be a viable choice for you.

• Are you adopting to even out a family? Or to finally get a child of a certain sex—perhaps that little girl you've always wanted after three boys? If so, examine your expectations care-

19

fully. Do you see your little girl dressed in ribbons and frills, your little boy in cowboy suits? What if you end up with a baseball player with braids, or a son who likes ballet?

One of the advantages of adopting is that you do have some choice instead of only chance when it comes to the sex of your child. But make sure you are not basing your choice on expectations that your child may not share and could come to resent.

• Are you adopting a "playmate" for your child? If you plan to adopt a child close in age to another of your children so they can "play together," consider some realistic possibilities. The adopted child and the one you have now may have entirely different interests, and your adopted child may gravitate to one of your other children or to a neighborhood child, leaving Johnny right where he was before. If you are adopting solely to provide a playmate, stop right here. It is both cheaper and wiser to send your child to nusery school, camp, scouts, or wherever. A child is not a commodity to be acquired like a toy at a store. He should be valued for himself, not for what he can provide to someone else.

Of course, in deciding what type of child best fits into the family, considerations involving the other children do play a major and even crucial part. The adopted child also may prefer to have someone in the family near his age. It's just that the "playmate" angle should not be the only factor.

Once you decide to adopt an "older" child, the next question is how old he should be. In the past, adoption agencies have recommended that you never adopt a child older than the eldest child already in your family or even the same age as one of your children. The main reason was that you would be disturbing the family's "birth order," particularly the special position of being the oldest child.

While that concept still is followed in many cases, it no longer is considered inviolable. Many parents who adopted a child older than their eldest son or daughter have discovered that—despite some highly competitive moments—there was a positive rather than a negative reaction by the "displaced" oldest child. Having a big brother or sister took away some of the pressure to always be the leader and set an example for the other children in the family.

Whatever the age of an adopted child, the potential reactions of the other children should be taken into account before the adoption is made. As silly as it sounds, even the most secure child may want extra reassurance that her parents are not going to disappear like the biological parents of the newly adopted brother or sister.

If you have children old enough to understand about adoption, you may want to sound them out about your plans before you make a final decision. If you get a negative response, find out whether they have misconceptions or hidden fears about adoption, or whether there are other problems you will have to deal with before adding another child. With younger children, it may be best to withhold the information until plans are firm because long delays can be too frustrating for them.

Finally, some people tend to either favor biological kids because they are "my own" and arrived first, or to overindulge adopted children in an effort to "be fair." Neither is a healthy way to raise your bio–adopted family. Consider the parenthood perspective of actor Charlton Heston, who has one biological child and an adopted one. Whenever anybody asks whether it is his son or daughter who is adopted, Heston always tells them: "Sometimes I forget which."

The Single Parent

If you are single, you are going to have a more difficult time adopting children than almost anyone else. Agencies will want to know about your stability, why you haven't married, why you want to adopt without getting married, why you think you can raise a child alone, and dozens of other things that you may feel are nobody's business but your own. Also, they usually will not consider you for any children except those for whom there are no couples available.

The adoption agencies want to be certain that single people are not adopting because they cannot establish meaningful relationships with the opposite sex or because they are lonely individuals who need someone on whom to lavish love and attention. Agencies are looking for people who have full and meaningful lifestyles, who have positive self-images, and who have both emotional security and, to some extent, financial security.

For these reasons, adoption agencies tend to favor prospective single parents in their thirties or forties who are content to "settle down" with a child and enjoy the daily routines of domestic living. However, they want parents who are energetic enough to see a child through young adulthood because raising a child, especially for a single person, can be an exhausting and time-consuming task.

Still interested? If so, it will be an uphill battle just getting an agency to consider you for a homestudy. So be sure adoption is what you really want. Before approaching an agency, make sure you have all of your references and resources together. This extra preparation often will make the difference between getting in the door and remaining out in the cold.

You specifically should be ready to answer these questions:
• Do you have relatives or close friends you can depend on for an extended family relationship?

Some sort of family-type relationship is important for your child's social development, and it also can provide support in times of crisis. The "family" could be other single friends, married couples, or relatives. Relationships with adults of the opposite sex from yourself are especially important to your adopted child.

In case you should die or be incapacitated, your child should have a legal guardian willing to raise her or him. This

22

may be unpleasant to think about, but it is necessary for the welfare of your adopted child. Since you have no marriage partner, you also should be prepared to have your insurance policies and will changed to specifically name your child as beneficiary.

Primarily, adoption agencies will want to know if you have good, healthy relationships with family and friends. If you cannot form such relationships, you probably could not establish one with an adopted child.

• Do you have adequate plans for caring for your child?

Children demand a great deal. For a single parent, these demands mean special arrangements and possibly a substantial change in your lifestyle. You might have to move from the city to the suburbs to get more room. You may have to move to an apartment or house closer to schools, parks, and other children. Day care, babysitting, or housekeepers have to be arranged. So do medical care, recreational opportunities, and transportation. All these points lead to the next question: money.

• Do you have the finances to raise a child alone?

Many adoption agencies require that single applicants be especially secure financially with a job that is steady, well-paying, and stable. The extra expenses that a single parent faces can be staggering. He or she is used to a budget that includes only one person, not two. More specific financial requirements will be discussed later in this book.

• Do you have the emotional and physical resources that child-raising requires?

Raising kids is a 24-hour-a-day, seven-day-a-week job. Adding a child to the life of a single person means a need for tremendous adjustments by both child and parent. You should consider whether a child will deprive you of the relationships and experiences you deem important. And you should ask yourself if you can give the extra love, attention, and support that the adopted child of a single parent will need.

Make no mistake about it. Being raised by a single parent

poses social and emotional problems for an adopted child. You will have to be able to help your child adjust to new surroundings at the same time you are helping her or him to cope with the idea of having only one parent. Many other people will be curious about your personal life. Some will assume that a lone woman with a child must be an unwed mother with an illegitimate child, or that a man alone with a child is divorced or widowed. You are the one who will have to help your child make sense of the reactions, suppositions, and prejudices of others, particularly when you are of different racial or national backgrounds.

As a single person, your decision to adopt is not an easy one. The child placed with a single parent frequently is a child considered difficult to place. Such a child may have emotional scars that take a long time to heal. It is ironic that single parents, who have the difficult job of raising children alone, often are given the children who need the most help.

Today the major qualification for prospective adoptive parents, married or single, with or without children, is that they have the potential for helping children develop into sound and mature adults. In the final analysis, only you can decide whether you are ready to enter into a life-long commitment to a relationship that becomes more complex as times goes on: the relationship between a parent and a child.

2

Children for Adoption

The adoption picture has changed dramatically in recent years. Not long ago, there were more young adoptable children waiting for parents than there were people willing to adopt them. Now the situation is reversed. The supply of such children, especially white infants, is far short of the demand.

Since 1970 the number of reported child adoptions in the United States has dropped sharply. About 175,000 children were adopted that year, but adoptions fell to about 169,000 in 1971, the last year for which official statistics are available. The Children's Bureau of the U.S. Department of Health, Education and Welfare estimates that placements have since dipped to about 140,000 a year. And about half of all adoptions involve children adopted by relatives.

Adoption officials cite several factors to explain the sharp decrease in the number of young children, particularly infants, available for adoption. One is the increased use of birth-control pills and other contraceptives. Liberalized abortion laws also account for part of the decline. And due to changes in social attitudes, more unmarried mothers are deciding to keep their babies. In the past, about 90 percent of the children

25

released for adoption by nonrelatives were born out of wed-
lock, but officials say that figure has declined.

The short supply of adoptable babies has its adverse effects.
Couples who cannot have children biologically are having to
wait longer to adopt a baby. One result is a reported upsurge
in "black market" adoptions by which anxious couples may
pay up to $35,000 to illegally adopt a baby. These operations
involve profit-seeking middlemen who seek out unwed mothers, doctors, lawyers, or social workers and offer them large
cash sums for providing babies for their clients. No matter
how desperate you may be to adopt, the black market is the
wrong place to find a baby. It is, in effect, the selling of a child
to the highest bidder and usually involves falsification of birth
certificates and other records.

There also are "gray market" adoptions, which involve the
direct placement of a child through a doctor or lawyer instead
of by an agency. While these "independent" adoptions are
somewhat controversial in some areas, they are legal in all
states except Connecticut and Delaware. Such adoptions are
discussed in a later chapter in this book.

The shortage of adoptable babies has a positive side, too.
Adoption agencies suddenly are finding a demand for children
who previously were considered unadoptable or "hard to
place." These are older children, black or other minority children, and handicapped children. More and more people are
willing to consider adopting such children. Ten years ago,
interracial children were rarely adopted. Today there are long
waiting lists for such children in many areas.

The tight adoption market also has focused new attention
on foster children. Despite what you might think from movies,
there are few "orphans" at children's institutions. Most children who lose one or both of their parents are cared for, and
often adopted, by relatives. Most children in institutional care
are foster children who cannot be released for adoption because their biological parents (or parent) will not give the

needed consent or, in some cases, because one of the parents cannot be located. Many of these children have been abandoned for all practical purposes. But as long as a parent keeps up even infrequent contact, in some states the child cannot be adopted. At best, he or she will be shuttled from one foster home to another.

With more people willing to adopt such children, the courts and many state legislatures have started to take a closer look at the situation of foster children. Laws such as the 24-month review in New York State are forcing adoption agencies and foster-care officials to consider what is in the best long-term interests of the foster child. This law requires that, after 24 months in foster care, a judicial review of a child's case must be made to determine if the child should return to his or her original home or be released for adoption. If the biological parents have no perceivable intention or plans to take care of the child, the child no longer need be left in limbo and can be released for adoption.

As a result of similar action in many states, more foster children, who previously would have remained unadopted and without permanent families, are now being released for adoption. Also, increasing numbers of children are being released for adoption who were previously considered unadoptable or hard to place: older, black, minority, and handicapped children.

So there are still children waiting to be adopted, including an ever dwindling number of infants. Children cannot be arranged like computer cards and filed away in neat piles. But there are certain "categories" of adoptable children we can discuss. If you are considering adopting a particular type of child, don't skip to the section that interests you most. Instead, look at each category because you might find your convictions swayed, or strengthened, about the child you think is just right for you.

The Infant

A cuddly, recently born baby girl or boy traditionally has been the goal of most adoptive parents. In 1966 nearly 90 percent of all nonrelative adoptions involved children under one year of age. That percentage has steadily declined with the decrease in the number of available infants, but it remains high. Most applicants for infant adoption traditionally have been childless or infertile couples. Perhaps infants are thought to be closest to the child such couples might have given birth to, or too young to have grown attached to any other parent figure.

But since there are fewer infants, and toddlers, around for adoption today, the adoption of a baby will take significantly longer than the adoption of any other age child. In some areas, if you have qualifications about the type of baby you want, it may take longer than five years of waiting—if you can find an agency or private intermediary willing to help you at all.

If you are more flexible about what you want in a child, or if you are adopting a minority child, if you are willing to accept a child with a medical problem or a handicap, or you just may be able to adopt a baby or toddler within two years or so. Parents who belong to minority groups—such as black, Indian, and Spanish-speaking couples—will have an easier time.

The wait for the placement of an infant is long and filled with the uncertainty that maybe you'll never get a baby. If you decide that only an infant will satisfy your needs, you should think carefully about what the adoption of a baby will mean to your individual lifestyle. Ask yourself the following questions:

• Is your life full and satisfying enough to occupy you while you wait? Do you have the patience to wait?

• If you are adopting for reasons of infertility, will a long

28

wait aggravate insecurities you may have about your sterility? Will it cause friction between you and your spouse?

• If you are in your late thirties or forties, and settled into a comfortable, babyless home life, will an infant really fit into your lifestyle comfortably?

• Do you really understand the responsibilities a baby brings? The diapers, illness, feedings, and crying? Or are you romantically involved with the idea of the ideal magazine advertisement baby who never cries or spits up?

One good way to test your feelings is to visit with friends or relatives who have children. Maybe you could volunteer to babysit for a weekend or a vacation period. This will give you some basis for a realistic decision about your way of living and how a child fits into that pattern. It also may help you decide whether you're really ready to enter into that long-term commitment known as parenthood.

Perhaps while you are searching for a baby you might consider an older child. But if only an infant will meet your particular needs, it might be better for both you and the older child if you waited; no child likes to be considered "second best."

The Older Child

The "older" child used to mean a child over six months old. It now means the child over six or, increasingly, even the child over nine years of age. While adoptions of older children are still outnumbered by infant adoptions, the 1970s have marked a rapid rise in placements of youngsters over six years old.

There are signs of a growing willingness by adoption applicants to consider other children besides infants. This is partly due to the shortage of adoptable babies. But it also reflects an increased acceptability by adoptive parents of the challenge of dealing with older children. The adoption of older children often is considered particularly advantageous for couples into or past middle age.

The American child who is past his first birthday usually has been in at least two other homes before placement in an adoptive family—his or her first home, and the agency institution or a foster home. Because of new foster care limitations and adoption laws in many states, young adoptable children remain in an agency nursery or foster home after birth without being adopted only if there have been unusual legal or medical problems. The exceptions might be children of school age, who may have been in care for a number of years under prior foster care regulations.

Children in the two-to-four age range often are harder to deal with initially than slightly older youngsters. Children at that age frequently do not take well to change, and they easily become disoriented and confused. They cannot fully comprehend or accept all that is happening to them, and they cannot verbalize their fears and anxieties very well. A proper climate of love and attention, plus time, usually will help such a youngster adjust to the difficulties involved in acquiring a new mommy and daddy.

An older child may show insecurity by being "too good" or by being devious about his desires. Or he may be hostile and test you constantly. A child who has been shuttled from home to home may not understand why anyone would want to reach out to him, and he may try to prove his theory that you, like everyone else in his life, ultimately will reject him.

It takes extra doses of patience to show the school-aged child that you are firmly committed to this new relationship of adoption. You, as the adult, will have to give direction to this alliance. It may take time. But parents who have adopted older children often talk of the rewarding times when their children began to trust and share as part of a family. When

Dave and Ruth Arias adopted a ten-year-old son named Philip in 1972, he previously had been in eight foster homes and a children's institution. Not surprisingly, Philip was a bundle of insecurities and it showed—he did poorly in school, he told tall tales about his past, and he displayed a general unsureness about becoming a permanent part of his new family, which also included another adopted son and two biological sons.

"It used to be that anything you'd ask him, he'd immediately react by saying, 'It wasn't me,' " recalls Ruth Arias. "He was so afraid to make mistakes, to be rejected, that he wouldn't take any chances."

But the Ariases were patient with Philip. The turning point came after he had been with the family about eight or nine months.

"We were talking about why we named our older son, Dave, after my husband, and I mentioned that we had always loved the name Jonathan and had wanted to call one of our sons by that name," Mrs. Arias says. "Phil was quiet for a while. Then he asked hesitantly, 'Since nobody else has that name, could I still be called Jonathan?' " So Phil became Jon, a very important step for him—and for the Ariases.

"It was like a new beginning," says Jonathan (Philip) Arias, who has since learned a lot about belonging. And while Jon hasn't completely overcome ten years of neglect and insecurity, "he has certainly grown," agrees Mrs. Arias.

Here are some questions to ask yourself if you are considering adopting an older child:

•   Can you accept the possibility that it may take time before you may be able to show love for your new child? That there may be things about each other you may not even like at first?

You and your adopted child approach each other as strangers—each with different experiences and habits, with different fears and expectations. It may take a while to get used to each other, and longer still to learn to like each other. You cannot expect instant love by either the parent or the child.

Both of you probably will have habits that are annoying to one another. But just as you don't expect to completely change your way of behavior overnight because it may not be what your new child is used to, you cannot expect your child to instantly change his habits because they may not fit in with your ways of doing things. You should be flexible enough to deal with your adopted child's insecurities and behavior problems in a way that will help him or her build a positive self-image. This is the ability to dislike the behavior but still like the child—and to get that distinction across to him.

• Can you bring yourself to seek professional help if needed?

You and your child might need outside advice and aid in working out aspects of your relationship. An older child may have emotional problems implanted long before he or she ever came into your home, and it is no reflection on your ability as a parent if you cannot fully cope with some of them. Rather than being a mark of failure, a decision to seek professional guidance can be the most mature action you can take as a responsible parent.

• Can you accept the fact that your child has had past experiences you can never fully share with him?

Many older children will talk endlessly about the good times they had at previous homes. The stories may or may not be exaggerated, but they are the only past your child may have to cling to and the only security if something should go wrong in his new surroundings. On the other hand, some adopted children cannot talk about their past because it is too painful emotionally. You may never know what caused certain attitudes or feelings.

In summary, "older" children come in a variety of ages and with a variety of challenges. They need parents who can meet most of those challenges and be enriched by them, parents who can teach them they are worthy of someone's love.

The Child with Special Needs

A child with special needs may be a child with a medical problem; a physical, emotional, or mental handicap; or a child with easily correctable problems, such as crooked teeth or a lisp. Generally, such children need extra attention, extra resources, and extra capable parents. They may not require extra financial resources, however. In many states there are adoption subsidies available or foundation funds that can be tapped. Children with special needs do not necessarily require financially well-off parents because these funding sources can provide the needed services or equipment at little or no cost. What these children need are parents with the patience, time, and understanding to deal with their problems.

Pity cannot be a motivating factor in the adoption of a child with a handicap. If you adopt a child because you feel sorry for him, you are giving him the added handicap of a crippled spirit. Parents of a special child need to be able to see something of value in their child and to be proud of his accomplishments. Here are some questions to consider if you are thinking about adopting a child with special needs:

• Will this child be a "second choice"?

Despite the increased flexibility of applicants for adoptions, the demand for children with physical or emotional problems isn't as great as for infants or older children without such problems. Many couples who are adopting their first child simply don't feel ready to take on added responsibilities in their first plunge into parenthood. As a result, the waiting period to adopt a child with special needs may be a good bit shorter than for children in greater demand. You might be tempted to request a child with special needs in order to avoid a long wait for an adoptive child or after you already have spent a lengthy time on a waiting list. Avoid that temptation. Children should be wanted because of their worth as human

33

beings, not because they happen to be the most convenient alternative to a first choice.

• Do you have a healthy attitude toward the particular problem of a particular child?

If you haven't had experience with this type of condition before, contact medical or psychological specialists for specific information. If possible, talk to parents of children with similar problems. These parents can fill you in on the intangible aspects of raising such children, and they usually have a realistic viewpoint concerning children with handicaps. The more you understand and accept the condition, the more secure you will be in dealing with it. You will have to help your child adjust to the realities of his situation, including both his potential and his limitations.

• Do you have the patience, tolerance, and ability to deal with frustration?

Both you and your family should consider the strains that a child of special needs may put on you all. Prospective parents of a special child should be able to accept the limitations of their child willingly and be prepared to cope with them. Such parents must be able to give without expecting to receive in return in many cases. Every family member should be in agreement that the adopted child will be an asset to the family, and not a liability.

• Are there resources available to help you deal with your child's special needs?

After you determine what it is your child needs (and that isn't always easy), you should check local hospitals, schools, clinics, and other organizations for programs that can be of service to your family in dealing with those needs. Your state, county, and local social service departments can tell you if there are any financial subsidies you can draw on for help. But if you live in a rural area, far from clinics or schools, you may have difficulty obtaining special services that may be necessary for a child with an emotional, mental, or physical problem.

You also should determine if the physical setup of your own home and neighborhood would present any problems to your adopted child. For example, if you live in a community of old two-story houses and three-story schools, a child with an orthopedic handicap such as polio might have a difficult time getting around.

The decision to adopt a child with special needs calls for some objective thinking on your part. A child with special needs requires special parents. Not altruistic parents who want to help an unfortunate child. And not "super parents" who can easily handle every problem. A child with special needs requires parents who realize what they are getting into, and who are willing to accept their child for what he is and for what he can be.

Adoption and Race

Until a few years ago, the chances of a nonwhite child being adopted were relatively poor. But that part of the adoption picture, too, has changed dramatically.

In 1970 for every 100 white children needing homes, there were 116 homes available. But for every 100 nonwhite children, there were only 39 homes. The majority of these nonwhite children were black or interracial. One short year later in 1971 there were 141 homes for every 100 adoptable white children, but the number of homes for every 100 nonwhite children had increased even more sharply to 79. Those trends generally have continued. Today nonwhite infants are as much in demand, and short supply, as white babies. However, there still is a shortage of applicants for older black children.

One reason for the change is that adoptions by black families have risen substantially in the past decade. Previously, blacks traditionally had shunned agency adoptions, although "unofficial" adoptions without legal formalities were common within many black communities. The reluctance to deal with agencies was partly due to the image of adoption agencies as white establishment bureaucracies. Also, many black families simply did not meet the financial requirements of agencies. In recent years, many adoption agencies have moved to attract black adoptive parents by hiring more black social workers and by publicizing the availability of children for black couples. Financial requirements have been eased. And some communities have established agencies dealing only with placements of black children in black homes. For example, Homes for Black Children in Detroit works exclusively with black applicants to place waiting black children. It makes an effort to keep the atmosphere relaxed and congenial, with rules and red tape kept to a bare minimum.

Another reason more nonwhite children are being adopted is a fairly recent phenomenon of placing minority children in white homes. This is especially true of biracial children who had one black parent and one white parent. Up until a few years ago, more than one third of all adopted black children also were going to white homes. Such transracial adoptions were rare until the late 1960s and early 1970s. They surged as a result of changing attitudes on the part of both adoption agencies and the public.

The big change by adoption agencies was that many began to ease a once rigid tradition of "matching" a child's nationality, physical appearance, and intellectual potential to the adopting parents. Back when adoptable infants were plentiful and homes were few, adoptive children were supposed to be as close as possible to the biological children that infertile couples couldn't have. The emphasis on matching continued until the late 1960s when more families besides infertile couples began applying for adoption and when the number of white infants released for adoption began shrinking. Since the majority of applicants were white, there were not enough white babies to meet the demand in many communities. At the same time, there was a growing awareness of the needs of "hard-to-adopt" children, including minority children. Many agencies gradually began to move away from physical matching to finding families with the inner qualities necessary to adopt a waiting child of any racial background.

Meanwhile, a liberalization of American racial attitudes had made interracial adoptions more acceptable. The groundwork for such adoptions was laid in the decade following the Korean War when over 3,000 Korean and Korean-American children were adopted into American homes. During the same time, several hundred American Indian children were placed for adoption outside Indian reservations, predominantly in white homes, under a joint project of the Bureau of Indian Affairs and the Child Welfare League of America.

In the past couple of years, however, the adoption of non-white children by white parents has run into a new controversy. In 1972 the National Association of Black Social Workers issued a statement condemning the practice of transracial adoptions as a way of finding homes for black children. Their statement said in part:

"We have taken the position that Black children should be placed only with Black families whether in foster care or for adoption. Black children belong physically, psychologically, and culturally in Black families in order that they receive the total sense of themselves and develop a sound projection of their future. Human beings are products of their environment and develop their sense of values, attitudes, and self-concept within their family structures. Black children in white homes are cut off from the healthy self-development of themselves as Black people."

The group argued that adoption agencies should do more to attract black adoptive couples by publicizing the new flexibility in agency standards, especially financial standards, and by recruiting in the black communities to find black homes for black children. (Similarly, a caucus of American Indians has filed lawsuits challenging the placing of Indian children with white families on grounds that such interracial adoptions amount to "genocide" of Indian tribes.)

Partly due to the increased opposition of some black groups to the adoption of black children by white parents, the number of such adoptions dropped nearly 40 percent in 1972 compared with 1971, according to a survey by the Boys and Girls Aid Society of Oregon. But this decrease was not offset by an increase in adoptions of black children by black families. Instead, black placements also dropped slightly. Adoption officials speculate that the slackening in the number of adoptions by black people may be the result of increased financial problems as the result of inflation and increasing unemployment, which tend to hit lower-income minority groups the hardest. But adoptions by black families still are up substantially from five or ten years ago.

The debate over whether or not nonwhite children should be placed in white homes has yet to be settled. In some communities, adoption agencies refuse to place black children with white parents, or at least strongly discourage it. Agencies in other communities take the view that an interracial home is better than no home for a black child if there aren't enough black applications. Many adoption officals and other professionals, including some blacks, fear that insistence upon placement according to racial or ethnic matching—such as black children to black homes only or Mexican children to Mexican homes only—will return adoption to the old matching system of blue-eyed children to blue-eyed parents and deny countless children a chance for permanent homes because there are not enough of the "right" families immediately available for each child who needs a home. In Texas, controversy arose when a black couple tried, and ultimately succeeded, in adopting their Mexican American foster son.

Generally, adoption agencies in the United States today will first seek a family of the same ethnic background for children who are black, Oriental, Indian, or Hispanic. But more adoptive parents from minority groups are needed. If you are black, you likely will have a better chance of finding an adoptable child sooner than your white counterpart, especially if you are interested in a young child.

Parents considering adopting across racial lines should think carefully about their decision and be committed to the idea before approaching an agency. Studies of parents who have successfully adopted interracially show that these parents have certain characteristics in common. They are independent people with a great deal of self-confidence and maturity; they tend to be flexible and willing to accept differences. Although some of the adopters have liberal or idealistic viewpoints, they do not view their adoption of a child of a different race as a charitable act or a step taken to defy prevailing social codes. Instead, according to these studies, such people see the child as the important consideration in the adoption; their adopted child is important to them because of his or her value as a human being, as their son or daughter, not because of skin color or physical characteristics.

International Adoptions

Although international adoptions account for a relatively small percentage of total adoptions in the United States, they have quadrupled since the end of World War II to an annual rate of more than 3,100 a year. In the 1970s the availability of adoptive children from other countries has begun to be outstripped by a rapidly growing demand as more prospective parents—faced with long waiting times and a shrinking supply of infants in the United States—turn to international adoptions.

Five years ago most international adoption agencies had

several adoptive children available for each application they received. Today many agencies have waiting lists for young children, and some no longer accept such applications. Like their U.S. counterparts, many international agencies report an overabundance of applications for infants and preschool children, and they say most applicants prefer girls over boys. As a result, many such agencies are asking prospective parents to consider slightly older children, particularly boys, or children with medical or physical problems.

Most children available for adoption from outside the United States are in developing countries. Virtually none are available from Western Europe or Scandinavia. There are formal adoption programs in Korea, South Vietnam, the Philippines, South America, and in Canada for Canadian Indian children. Independent adoptions, which aren't handled through an agency, can be arranged in Bangladesh, Africa, South America, India, and the Far East. There is a growing number of independent adoptions of children from South America, primarily from Ecuador, Costa Rica, Nicaragua, Guatemala and Colombia.

International adoptions are discussed more fully in a later chapter of this book. International agency programs and some other contacts are listed in the directory. But if you are interested in adopting a child from abroad, you first should consider the following questions:

    • Do you want to adopt a child from another country for humanitarian reasons? Or because the idea of your own international family sounds exotic?

You may be drawn to children in a particular country because of some publicity about the problems of homeless children there. But your concern alone is not a sufficient reason to consider adopting one of the children. As in any adoption, your child should be wanted for herself, not just because you want to "save" her from some miserable fate. Also beware of adopting a child because he represents an exciting cause or an interesting adventure. You are adopting a child, not a tropical houseplant to put in the living room.

On the other hand, an international adoption can be a positive consideration if you like children and want to consider those from other countries who are in need of homes.

• Will a child from another country, who may be racially different from you, be accepted in your community?

Naturally, you first should ask yourself whether *you* can accept a child racially and physically different from yourself. But you also should consider the reactions of neighbors and others in the community, as well as others in your family. This should not rule your decision to adopt a foreign-born child, but you and your child will have to deal with such people daily and you should be prepared for potential problems. If there is a strong local prejudice about people with the child's racial or ethnic background, will it be unfair to subject the child to the likely consequences? Also think about whether or not your child will be the only child of his heritage in your community and in school. If there are no other families with children like your adopted child, will yours have to face being known as the "different one"?

If major problems are likely to arise, you may be faced with one of two choices—moving to another neighborhood or community, or considering another type of child to adopt.

• Can you accept a complete lack of information about your child's parents, home life, illnesses, and perhaps even his true date of birth?

In some countries, younger children often are left at orphanages or abandoned in public places without any documents or information about where they came from. This means you will probably never know anything about such an adoptive child other than perhaps brief reports about his behavior at the orphanage. With older children, bits and pieces about the past often spill out when they master English, but there will always be gaps.

41

You may have to help your child come to grips with uncertainties about his origin. Many adoptive parents start "baby books" for their foreign-born children—including school-age children—that begin with pictures of the child's arrival and first days in his new home. The books also may include postcards and other items from the child's native country as well as any correspondence involving the adoption. This can help a child feel there are roots to hold onto in life.

There are many reasons for adopting a child from another country. The important point to remember is that international adoption is not a rescue mission or simply a way to provide American couples with young children unobtainable in the United States. Such adoptions may accomplish both ends. But the primary objective of adoption across national boundaries is to provide homeless children with loving, permanent homes unavailable in their homelands.

Children for Adoption: A Summary

If your heart is set on adopting an infant or toddler, you will be in for a long and perhaps frustrating wait. The average wait for a healthy white infant in the United States is at least five years—if you can find an agency willing to accept your application in the first place. Black couples seeking black babies or any couples wishing to adopt a child of mixed race will face shorter waits, but fewer babies of any race are being released for adoption. Many couples are turning to international adoptions, where the wait for an infant or toddler takes up to two years.

Despite the decreasing supply of adoptable babies—and the controversies over interracial adoptions—there still are thousands of children in the United States and abroad who need homes each year. These are older children, especially black or racially mixed children, and youngsters with physical or men-

42

tal handicaps. More and more adoptive parents are seeking out such children, and the waiting time at present generally ranges from about six months to a year and a half.

Yet adoption agencies in many states still have to recruit parents for older children. For example, the New York State Board of Social Welfare signed up an advertising agency to mount a public service ad campaign about the rewards of adopting older and other "hard-to-place" children. You might want to consider the theme line from the ads: "Have a child. It's as beautiful as having a baby."

3

Agencies and Homestudies

You've made up your mind. You have looked at this question of adoption from all sides and you have decided that, yes, I want to adopt a son or a daughter. And that decision raises new questions. Such as, how do you start? And where do you turn?

The first step is to decide if you want to adopt through an adoption agency or if you want to try to arrange a nonagency, or independent, adoption. Basically, there are three types of adoption agencies: public agencies, which usually are run by county or city departments of welfare or social services; private agencies, which place a broad range of homeless children; and sectarian agencies, which specialize in adoptions for children and parents of specific religions such as Jewish, Catholic, or Lutheran, although some may place across religious lines.

Independent adoptions usually are arranged through lawyers or doctors. These are the "gray market" or, in some cases, the "black market" adoptions you have heard about. Before you opt for the independent route, make sure you understand how adoption agencies work today. You may find that certain assumptions you may have about the rigidity and requirements of agencies no longer hold true. If you find that, for whatever reason, you cannot work with an agency, consider very carefully the information on independent adoptions in Chapter Five of this book. (International adoptions, which are discussed in Chapter Six, operate via both agencies and independent contacts.)

More than 75 percent of all adoptions in the United States are agency adoptions. One reason is the increased flexibility of adoption agencies in recent years. Another is the greater assurance of legal safeguards with an agency adoption. Adoption agencies in most states are licensed and regulated by state governmental bodies such as a department of public welfare or a department of social services. These departments set legal standards that adoption agencies must follow to keep their licenses. For example, to avoid the possibility that an adopted child could be taken away from you by a biological parent, there are steps such agencies must take to ensure that a child has been legally released for adoption. In addition to legal protections, agencies also provide a screen of anonymity between the bio parents and adoptive parents, whereas in some private adoptions you might come into contact with a bio parent. Agencies also are able to provide preadoption guidance for parents *and* children, as well as postadoption guidance for adopted children and their parents.

In a few states there is no specific adoption licensing. However, all states do have certain standards that are followed, and there are efforts under way in some of the states to institute legal guidelines for agency adoptions (as well as for independent adoptions).

The policies and practices of adoption agencies across the country vary widely, so it is impossible to generalize about comparisons between public agencies and private ones. One type of agency is not necessarily "better" than another, contrary to an old wives tale that private agencies placed a "better class" of baby (whatever that meant) than public ones. A

45

private agency adoption usually will cost more than a public agency placement, but about all adoption agencies today have one thing in common: a severe shortage of infants and a resulting sharp decline in placements. For example, at the Los Angeles County Department of Adoption, the largest public agency in the United States, placements in 1973 dropped to about 1,100 children, from an annual rate of about 2,500 in the late 1960s. The private Spence-Chapin Adoption Service in New York City placed 110 youngsters in 1973, down from a high of 475 in 1967.

So the first thing you want to do is to find an agency that will accept your application to adopt a child and will put you on a waiting list for a homestudy. What is a homestudy? It used to be an intense investigation by an agency into the intimate details of your private life and finances, with a social worker literally and figuratively peeking under your carpets. Or at least that was the way many adoption applicants felt after going through a homestudy. But today most agencies use homestudies, which usually include personal visits to your home by a social worker, as a way to help parents reach their own decisions about adoption rather than acting out the old stereotype of a homestudy as an opportunity for a minor inquisition. The homestudy is the final step before the search for a child to be placed in your home.

Finding an Agency

Okay, so how do you find an adoption agency and get a homestudy? Check the listing of state departments of public welfare and social services in the directory of this book and write to obtain an up-to-date listing of adoption agencies licensed in your state or county. Then sit down and start writing to agencies in your area to find out how to apply to adopt a child. Simply say you are considering adoption and ask for information about the adoption program and the children in need of homes at that agency. You need not list your preferences or include other personal information at this time. Also ask for the requirements or regulations for adoptive applicants.

Many agencies will simply send you a brochure or a printed pamphlet about their programs, but some may reply personally, enclosing an application form or other preliminary paperwork. They may even invite you to attend a group meeting for prospective applicants at the agency. That can be a good sign. But before you reply, you may want to talk to other parents who have recently worked with the same agency.

Each adoption agency has its own policies and standards, fees, requirements, basic philosophy, and availability of children. You may have to contact almost every agency in your area to find an agency handling the type of adoption that interests you. If you want an infant, you may have an especially hard time finding an agency that will encourage you to apply. Some people find that the most frustrating part of the preadoption process is not the actual homestudy but finding an agency that will at least put them on a waiting list for a homestudy.

You can take some steps to simplify your agency hunting by doing a little homework in advance. With proper information and preparation, you may be able to save yourself months of confusion and frustration. For example, you may be interested in an "older" child. In your mind, this means the wait for a homestudy and placement should be minimal. But you are surprised to find that the agency you contact will not even do a homestudy right away. First of all, it may be that your idea of an older child differs from the agency's. Perhaps "older" to you means a three-year-old, while to the agency "older" means six years of age and up, and there already is a backlog of applications for three-year-olds. Or it may be that the agency doesn't handle the type of child you requested. You

47

can save yourself some time and aggravation by finding out in advance what agency handles what type of applicant and what type of child.

Here are some suggestions on how to get in the door at an adoption agency:

• Find out what children actually are available for adoption in your area.

You can obtain this information by writing to various agencies or telephoning them. If you are interested in adopting an older child, a minority child, or other special children, ask for information about specific adoption programs for such children. The small investment in postage stamps or phone calls may pay large dividends in accurate, current information directly from the agencies. Secondhand gossip from friends or relatives may be inaccurate, out of date, or applicable only for certain couples dealing with certain agency workers. If you are willing to consider any available child, you may be able to get on a waiting list right away. If you cannot, or if the prospects for adopting soon in your area are dim, contact specialized agencies, local adoptive parents groups, and adoption exchanges listed in the directory to this book about sources of children outside your area or state that an agency can tap. An agency's staff members may be more willing to speak to you if they know they actually will be able to place a child with you in a reasonable length of time. Above all, don't accept the blanket statement, "There are no children." In 1972 Ursula Gallegher of the U.S. Department of Health, Education and Welfare's office of Child Development stated that there were an estimated 60,000 children awaiting adoption in the United States. Today some estimates range as high as 120,000, not including some of the 364,000 children in foster care potentially eligible for adoption.

• Decide which agency best fits your needs and request, in writing, that it do a homestudy for you.

Some agencies may send you an application for a home-

48

study and adoption in response to a phone request. Generally, however, agencies require a written request before they will consider you for a homestudy. If the agency is accepting applications, it will send you a form to fill out. Or it may invite you to the agency for an interview or a group meeting of prospective parents before you fill out your application. After you return your completed application to the agency, it will be reviewed and, if all goes well, you will be placed on a waiting list for a homestudy.

Again, when writing to request a homestudy, you do not have to go into a lot of detail about your adoption preferences. Just say you want to apply to adopt a child and state the general type, or types, you wish to consider. If you eventually are put on a waiting list for a homestudy, don't hesitate to call back at periodic intervals, "just to see how things are moving." Keep your name on the active list and don't let the agency forget you. Keep a record of all correspondence and dates of phone or personal contacts. If possible, insist that you get information directly from a supervisor or caseworker, not a secretary or receptionist.

• Personally contact the agency as well as writing or telephoning.

A face is much better remembered than a letter or voice. These days, adoption agencies get many phone calls and letters inquiring about adoption, many of them from people who may be curious about the adoption situation just in case they want to consider that parental alternative. A personal visit shows that you are serious about adopting. It also makes it harder for agency officials to refuse to at least consider your application. The goal of a personal visit, however, is not to put pressure on the agency but to encourage the agency to consider you as an individual who is sincerely interested in adopting a child of your own.

• Become active in an adoptive parents group.

Adoptive parents groups can be important sources of information on local agencies. You can compare notes with other people who have already adopted children or are at various stages of the adoption process. Group members likely will have had experience with several different agencies and they may be able to provide you with tips on how to approach certain agencies, what kinds of children are available at different agencies, and how you may be able to convince an agency to put you on the waiting list. Joining an adoptive parents group also shows you are serious about adoption. Besides, you might learn something.

Like agencies, adoptive parents groups operate under varying philosophies, so you'll have to check several groups to find out what activities they focus on. If you are adopting your first child, a group concerned with the problems of adopting a child into an existing family would not necessarily be helpful to you. The directory lists some of the known adoptive parents groups. Write to the one closest to you and ask about its program.

Sorry, No Children

If no local agency will accept your application, or if the wait seems unacceptably long, you may have to try locating an adoptive child on your own through agencies outside your state or community or via the adoption exchanges. How to go about that is discussed in the next chapter. You also might want to look at the chapters on independent adoptions and international adoptions.

Make sure, however, that you are not closing some doors yourself. Perhaps you would be considered by an agency if you were even slightly more flexible about the type of child you want. For example, although adoptive applicants today are less likely to seek the "perfect" child, some agencies complain that applicants who ask for girls far outnumber those who request boys. Nobody really knows if this is because girls may be considered "easier to handle" or if perhaps there still is a reluctance to have an adopted boy carry on a family name. Whatever the reason, couples who request only a girl may have to wait a year or two longer than couples who will accept a girl or a boy within the same age range.

If flexibility isn't your problem, maybe you have been calling the wrong department or talking with someone at the agency who doesn't have the authority to act on your adoption request. Maybe another personal visit to the agency might help you get a foot in the door. And there may be agencies you hadn't considered before, such as sectarian agencies of a faith different from yours. Check with parents who have dealt with these agencies before. Or with your own clergyman.

The Wisconsin Open Door Society gives this advice to prospective adoptive parents who keep running into closed doors:

1. Be patient, but persevere. Do not be afraid to repeat contacts with agencies to find out what is happening. You're going to put a lot of time and emotional energy into adopting.

2. Try to broaden your concept of an adoptable child as much as possible. Consider all the kids you feel you can really love and nurture in light of the kids who need *you*.

But don't take a child you really don't want. This is not a selfish attitude. It is best for you, and the child, if you find a child who meets your own concept of a son or daughter.

Agency Requirements

In order to be approved for adoption (or, in some cases, even to be put on a waiting list), there are certain basic adoption requirements that you will have to meet. These may vary

51

somewhat from agency to agency and from state to state. But some general requirements are outlined below.

AGE

In most states, adoptive parents must be at least twenty-one years old and can be no older than sixty-five. Agencies generally like to place children in homes where parents are less than forty years older than the adopted child but more than eighteen years older. They want parents who are young enough to see a child through young adulthood, yet old enough to establish a mature parent-child relationship. Some agencies will bend the rules in certain cases, such as in a family where one spouse is significantly older than the other. Or when there are close relatives—such as brothers or sisters of the parents—who could help take care of the child in the event that one or both parents became incapacitated or died.

Adoption agencies also like to consider the ages of any children already in the family, although there are no laws regulating this. Many agencies prefer that there be other children close in age to the adopted child rather than making him an "only child" because of a wide age gap.

MARITAL STATUS

Some agencies require that married couples be married at least two years before adopting. If you are divorced and remarried, you also will have to provide evidence that your divorce was legal and you may be asked why your previous marriage dissolved. Other agencies are more concerned about the stability of a marriage than the time length. They will try to determine, through the homestudy and by talking to your acquaintances, if your marital relationship is one of mutual respect and cooperation. Such agencies do not demand total marital bliss. Indeed, they may assume that two people who never quarrel never really communicate. What they are looking for is evidence that your marriage has the potential for growth despite a few disagreements now and then.

Single parents are more acceptable as adoptive parents today than in the past. Agencies look for an individual who has shown an ability to form warm, meaningful friendships, and they will closely check references to determine this ability. If you are single and divorced, you also will have to document that your divorce was legal and you may have to discuss your previous marriage.

FINANCES

The amount you earn is not as important as your ability to adequately manage on that amount. Only a very few agencies will require that you have a specific amount of savings or that you own your own home. At least half the states have some form of adoption subsidy available, sometimes with preference given to lower-income families or to foster parents who adopt foster children released for adoption after being placed in that foster home. There also are medical subsidies available for children with special needs, regardless of income.

The cost of adoption to you can vary widely. Generally, the total cost of adopting through an agency, including agency fees and legal fees, ranges from about $200 to more than $2,000. For independent adoptions, the cost usually is higher, ranging from $1,500 to more than $3,500, partly because the adoptive parents usually must pay the medical costs of the biological mother. (Black market prices can go as high as $25,000 or more.) International adoptions can cost anywhere from $250 to more than $2,500.

Many agencies will waive part or all of their regular fees for low-income families or families that adopt hard-to-place children. An increasing number of companies also are offering adoption benefits to employees to cover part of the cost of adoption. Financial requirements, adoption subsidies, and benefits and adoption costs are discussed in detail in Chapter Seven of this book.

HEALTH

The adoption agency you decide to work with will ask you to have a medical examination by your family physician, who will either fill out special health forms supplied by the agency or send the agency a letter describing your physical condition. If you are a childless couple, and it isn't known if either of you is infertile, you may be required to undergo fertility tests before an agency will accept your application for an infant or a toddler. Generally, agencies are reserving such youngsters for parents who cannot have children biologically.

If you have a medical problem, such as diabetes or a heart condition, or a physical handicap, the agency will ask you to provide specific information to show that it would not interfere with your potential to raise a child. Some agencies have conscious, or unconscious, prejudices about such things. If you have a health problem or a handicap, you may have to blaze a lonely trail, forcing agencies to look at you as a parent with limits, not a limited parent.

Adoption agencies traditionally have considered handicapped parents only for children with the same handicap. Groups like the National Association for Handicapped Parents have fought for acceptance of the idea that many handicapped people have the extra capabilities and resources needed to raise a nonhandicapped child. Some nonhandicapped children are being placed with handicapped parents, but still on a very limited basis.

RELIGION

Until recent years, most states strictly enforced laws requiring that adopted children be placed in homes of the same religious background as one of the child's biological parents. In essence, this meant that, if the child's mother was Catholic, the child was assumed to be Catholic. If she was Protestant, the child was assumed to be Protestant. And so forth. At one time, if the mother's religion wasn't known, children often were randomly assigned a faith when they came into an agency's care—baby No. 1 was Protestant, baby No. 2 was Catholic, and baby No. 3 was Jewish. Black children were assumed to be Protestant, and Puerto Rican and Italian children were assumed to be Catholic.

About three fourths of the states still have laws on the books requiring that a child be placed in a home of the same religious faith "when possible." It is the phrase "when possible," or some similar legal wording, that is getting attention today. Some agencies are interpreting this to mean that it is better to place a child in a home of a different religion from that of the biological mother than for the child to remain in an institution. The Civil Liberties Union and other groups are seeking to change the religious matching laws. But meanwhile such laws can influence placement of children. Individual judges may interpret the law as they see fit. Some consider such laws as "blue laws" and determine that the phrase "when possible" allows placement across religious lines. Other judges take a stricter view of religious requirements.

Most states also still require adoption applicants to belong to an established religion. Here again, there have been court battles to establish the right of applicants without established religious affiliations or beliefs to adopt children. But changes have been slow. However, religious requirements generally are not as strict as they once were. For example, most nonsectarian agencies don't require adoptive parents to be active or practicing members of a church. You should check the religion requirements for adoptive parents in your area with local agencies or adoptive parents groups. The first thing many prospective parents do when they apply to adopt is to start going to church regularly, only to find later that their case worker may not even ask about church. But, of course, there can be other benefits. One adoptive father reported back at an adoptive parents meeting: "You people had me so scared about the religious references required that I went back to temple. And, you know, it's not bad." He now serves on the temple board and his adopted son attends religious education classes his wife teaches.

Evaluating an Agency

Just as an adoption agency will evaluate your potential as a parent, you should check the policies and competence of the agency you will be dealing with. The American Academy of Pediatrics Committee on Adoption and Dependent Care has developed the following list of characteristics of a good adoption agency to help prospective adoptive parents evaluate social agencies:

1. An active board of directors or advisory committee that requires standards of practice and whose members are representative of all professions involved in adoption
2. Readiness to change or modify policies in line with new knowledge
3. Adequate staff composed of professional qualified social workers, supervisors, and an administrator
4. Medical decisions and medical staff work provided by qualified physicians, nurses, and allied health personnel
5. Legal decisions participated in by qualified attorneys

6. Existence of a cooperative spirit among all professional people involved

7. Licensing or approval by the appropriate state agency

8. Member of a national, standard-setting organization, such as the Child Welfare League of America

The easiest way to check these points is to go directly to the agency and ask for information in the form of annual reports, recommendations from other adoptive parents, or other material. You can personally visit the agency, particularly at semisocial events such as open houses or teas. You also can check with adoptive parents groups or the appropriate government agency in your area.

Documentation and References

Once you are accepted for a homestudy, you will be asked to provide documentation for certain basic information, such as your annual income and your marital status. Probably at the first meeting, your case worker will ask to see the following documents, if applicable to your case:

1. Marriage certificate
2. Divorce decrees
3. Birth certificates (for both parents and any children)
4. W-2 federal income tax form for the previous year
5. Bank statement
6. Insurance policies
7. Statement on holdings of any real property and stocks
8. Naturalization papers or visa

You usually will be asked to provide three to six personal references—friends or neighbors who can verify your potential to be good parents to an adopted child. The agency also may ask the name of your doctor and your clergyman. The agency may call or visit the people you put down as references. Or it may request a letter from each of your references or ask that they fill out a form.

Many agencies will not even consider anyone for adoption who has a criminal record or an other-than-honorable military discharge. Those that will study such people will require twice the amount of information as on other applicants, particularly regarding the circumstances of their past record and their rehabilitation since that time. If you are in this category, you will need more impressive references to verify your present exemplary behavior.

The Homestudy

The big day is here at last. You have filled out all the forms. You've had all the medical tests. You have attended the group meetings. After what seemed like forever, you are finally meeting with the social worker to begin the homestudy that, hopefully, will lead to the arrival of an adopted child into your family.

If you are like most prospective adoptive parents, your first homestudy visit at your home probably will be viewed with about as much apprehension as your first date. It likely will set off a flurry of frantic housecleaning the likes of which you haven't done since the last time your mother-in-law came to dinner. And, chances are, the social worker will calmly take coffee in the living room, never moving off the couch during the hour and a half he or she stays. Some wives feel so frustrated that they practically drag the caseworker bodily off the couch with a "but you must see the view from the kitchen." Or else the worker walks through the house, with anxious parents trailing, and says nothing more than, "Are you planning on moving soon?"

Some anxiety is understandable. After all, this social worker controls your parental destiny. What if he or she doesn't like your decor? In reality, superficial matters like decor and a little dust under the rug don't count. You want to make a good impression, of course. But the main purpose of a home visit is to see you relaxed on your home turf, not to catch you off guard with a skeleton in your closet.

If you are married, the social worker probably will want to see both spouses on the first visit. If you have other children, the social worker will want to see them, too. Don't worry if at times like this your kids seem to rally forth with their worst qualities. Adoption workers know that children are not always angels. One mother recommends getting lots of coffee cake for the occasion. "Not for your worker," she says. "To stuff in your kids' mouths when they become restless." Every time this mother's three-year-old began to whine during the home visit, she offered the child a piece of cake. The only problem, she adds jokingly, is that "this technique could backfire if your worker doesn't believe in between-meal snacks."

Homestudies can take from three or four weeks to three to six months. The time a study takes depends on the agency's policies, the caseworker's technique, and the personal needs of the prospective parents. Other factors can enter into the time length, such as vacations, retirement of a worker, the worker's experience in dealing with a particular type of adoption, and various delays in obtaining documents or forms. It is a good idea to ask the agency the "approximate" time range of the average homestudy. But be prepared for unexpected delays.

Some agencies have a set number of interviews. One common schedule is three interviews with the couple (with at least one of the interviews at the couple's home) and one interview with each spouse at the agency's offices. Other agencies are more flexible, preferring to set up a schedule according to the particular needs of the situation.

Don't be afraid to ask to set a date for the next meeting

before the interviews end. It may save you time and it also saves you the uncertainty of waiting days and weeks for the phone to ring or the mail to come with the next appointment date. Your anxiety level is high enough. If no date for your next appointment is set and you don't hear anything for a couple of weeks, don't be hesitant about calling your caseworker. It shows you are interested. Your caseworker will make an appointment in advance before visiting your home. Despite what you see in old movies, they don't make surprise house calls.

The home visits themselves generally are like casual conversations with a new acquaintance instead of some type of grilling about your views on adoption. During the conversation, the social worker will try to draw out your feelings about your marriage, your attitudes toward children, and your desires to adopt. Your worker probably will bring up in some form questions like these:

If married, do you have a satisfying marital relationship?
Why do you wish to adopt as a means to have children?
What type of child interests you, and why?
Is adoption a positive step for you?
Do you understand the problems of the type of child you are interested in?

Many adoptive parents say a homestudy can be very much like psychotherapy in that you are given the time and encouragement to explore your feelings in depth with a skilled professional. But if you feel there are areas you would like to keep private, areas you feel are not relevant to adopt, let your worker know. We all have things we prefer not to discuss with others.

Here are some suggestions some adoptive parents have found useful in approaching an adoption agency homestudy.

• Don't try too hard to impress a caseworker.

Just try to relax as much as you can in such a situation so that you and your worker can get to know each other. She or he wants to know you as you really are and is not looking for some kind of "superparent." You are a pretty special person, after all. Your worker just needs the opportunity to discover that.

• Don't lie to your worker.

There may be times when you want to stretch the truth a little, or bend things slightly so they are more favorable to you. But you will only get caught eventually in your stories, and that has to be worse than whatever it was you were trying to cover up.

• Don't try to prove you are the perfect couple with the perfect marriage.

You and your spouse are not Siamese twins. You are separate individuals married to each other, who respect and cooperate with each other. If you never disagree, it may mean that neither of you has the strength to function alone. Don't be afraid to tell your worker that you and your spouse have some spats from time to time. A little marital disharmony is necessary for communication in a marriage. And it makes the marriage a lot more interesting, too.

• Don't try to agree with everything your worker says.

For one thing, the worker may be playing the devil's advocate, throwing out things to see your reaction. Second, you are entitled to your own opinions. If your worker is a Republican and you are a Democrat, that's not going to stop him or her from approving your application.

• Do try to be prompt and to have the proper documents when they are requested. The fewer the delays in your homestudy, the faster you will know if you have been approved for an adoption.

What if you find during your interviews that you cannot get along with your worker, or with the agency? You have a couple of options. First, you can start with yourself. Is the relationship failing because of a problem you are having, and can you change that? If you cannot change alone, you may want to discuss the problem openly with your worker. This may seem like a hard thing to do. You probably don't want to make waves with the person who determines whether or not you get a child. But it is better to bring the problem out in the open rather than leave the worker guessing about what it is that is bothering you.

The same advice—to bring things out in the open—holds true if you decide the worker is at fault. If you cannot work things out, your second option is to ask for a different worker. This request should be made directly to the worker's supervisor or to the director of the agency. But you still should discuss the problem with the worker before you go to the superior. Do not attack the worker's competence; simply discuss the change rationally on the basis of "irreconcilable differences."

If all else fails, you can switch agencies. But that may leave you right where you started—at the bottom of a waiting list, if you can get on one at all. And you will have to explain to the new agency why you left the other agency in mid-homestudy. If you are certain your present agency is unworkable for you, check with other agencies about switching and give them your reasons. When you get a positive response from another agency, that is the time to inform the first agency you are switching. You may find the announcement that another agency has agreed to help you stirs the first one to take action to rectify situations you were not pleased with, and perhaps you won't have to switch after all. In any case, by checking things out in advance, you will not be left out in the cold.

In most cases, however, you won't run into such problems. Somewhere along the way your caseworker should tell you how she feels the homestudy is going and whether or not she will recommend placing a child with you. If you don't get the message, ask. Don't worry about being pushy. If she does have reservations, the sooner you know about them the better, to give you all the opportunity to discuss them fully.

When the study is completed, the caseworker will write up a final report. This is read by the staff members who place children and by supervisory personnel. It becomes part of your court record if the adoption is completed. The report is rarely seen by the prospective parent studied. The caseworker may tell the parent about the substance of the report and the final recommendation. But you, the prospective parents, usually will not get a copy.

The caseworker's final recommendation is based on the specific requirements of the agency, the availability of the type of child you are seeking, and the worker's general impression of you as prospective parents. Basically, agencies require a stable homelife where a child will fit in comfortably. But what constitutes "stable" is a subjective matter. It does mean, however, a home where a child will feel secure and loved.

What if you are not recommended for a child? Discuss the reasons for this with your worker and find out what you could do to reverse the decision. You may be told to wait, to receive counseling, or to consider a child other than the type you originally requested. If you are not told the reasons for the adverse decision, demand to be told. It is your right. If you cannot get satisfaction from your worker, continue up as high as you have to in order to get an answer—supervisor, administrator, government official. If you disagree with the decision, you have little recourse except in states or communities where agencies are subject to review boards or hearings. If you approach a second agency, you will have to give them the information that the first agency did not approve you.

If you are approved for a child placement after the homestudy—and most prospective parents are—you will get an official notification confirming the approval. You are then ready for the most important step—finding your child.

4

Locating a Child

Ideally, after you have been approved for an adoption, your caseworker soon will find a child she feels would be right for you. All you will have to do is wait impatiently for that phone call out of the blue telling you that a child may be waiting for you. The caseworker then will invite you to the agency to see a picture of the child or to meet the child. She also will give you some information on the child's background. If you are adopting an older child, the caseworker may arrange for you and the youngster to size each other up in the less official atmosphere of a park, museum, or zoo, rather than at the agency office. It is possible that you may feel the child is not right for your family; expressing doubts or even rejecting a placement does not jeopardize your chances of getting a child. If, however, you decide this is the child for you, your new son or daughter will be placed in your home.

But what if the weeks roll by and that phone call doesn't come and your agency tells you it may be many months before a child is found for you? Or what if you have not even been able to get on a waiting list because the agencies in your area say the type of children you are interested in are not available in large enough numbers?

If you are seeking a healthy infant or toddler, there is little you can do to speed the process because there simply are not enough children to meet the demand. Otherwise, there are two possible courses of action you can take: One, you can sit and wait for a year or two until a child is put in your arms or you finally are placed on a waiting list. Two, you can shorten the wait by becoming better informed about the children who actually are available for adoption, both in your area and elsewhere, and, if necessary, by trying to locate among these children a child who would fit into your life.

This can be helpful to your agency if you have been approved for adoption. If you haven't gotten that far, locating a child first may enable you to convince an agency to do a homestudy on you. Again, be sure that the problem isn't that you are limiting yourself by being inflexible about the type of child you will accept. The more flexible you are, the easier it will be for either you or your agency to locate a child for your family.

Whether or not you have been approved by an agency, probably the most reliable sources you can tap for information on available children are the adoption exchanges established by private organizations, parent and citizen groups, or state and city agencies. These exchanges list children who are waiting to be adopted, and some also list prospective parents who wish to adopt. Some groups generally list children for whom local agencies have had difficulty finding homes.

All the exchanges have the same purpose—to help children find homes that may not be readily available in the community or state where the child presently is located. And, second, to help prospective parents who cannot locate adoptable children in their own areas. Ed and Sharon Barco, for example, had been waiting for a baby for eight months after their homestudy was completed, and there seemed little likelihood that a child would be available from their agency in the near future even though the Barcos were willing to accept a hard-to-place child. Finally, the couple urged their caseworker to register them with the various exchanges. This was not done automatically in their state.

About another eight months later, through one of the exchanges, the Barcos located in a nearby city a sixteen-month-old boy with a heart defect. They were shown a picture of a slightly undersized baby with very large brown eyes. The child had been released for adoption less than two months before because his biological mother could not cope with the special needs of a child with a serious heart condition.

By consulting with their family doctor and a heart specialist he recommended, Ed and Sharon learned that the baby's heart condition was operable and that the baby would have a better than average chance for recovery and eventual normal activity. Their insurance would cover part of the surgical costs, and their agency assured them the state would pick up the remaining expenses as part of its medical subsidy plan for adoptive children. So the Barcos took into their home a son—Edward Harold Barco—whom they might never have found if they had not taken the initiative to expand their adoption search beyond their own community.

If you have been approved by an agency for adoption, and if the wait has been longer than three or four months with little prospect for a placement soon, make sure the agency has listed you with local, state, and national adoption exchanges. Your adoption worker should do this; if she has not, talk to her about it. Almost every state now has a central listing of children available for adoption, updated monthly according to current information from each licensed adoption agency in the state. Since 1970 California has used a computer to match adoptive children and families. There have been proposals in Congress to establish a computerized National Adoption Information Exchange to centralize such matching on a national scale through the Department of Health, Education and Welfare.

Whether or not you have completed a homestudy, you can directly contact groups that run exchanges for information on what children are available. Some groups, such as the Adoption Resource Exchange of North America (ARENA), regularly publish newsletters, sent to parent groups and agencies, containing descriptions of representative children listed with that exchange. Others, such as the Illinois Multiple Listing Service of the Child Care Association of Illinois, distribute in book form information on children available for adoption in specific geographic areas. Photographs and brief descriptions of waiting children are included in such books, which are periodically updated. You can obtain information about these newsletters and listings by writing directly to the groups that operate the exchanges; they are listed in the directory to this book. The newsletters and exchange books also may be available through local agencies or adoptive parents groups.

On page 68 you will find an example of a monthly listing of available adoptive children by one state adoption exchange.

The exchanges work on the same principle as multiple listing in real estate. The theory is that you can reach more prospective parents and benefit more children if you centralize and share information that can lead to these children finding homes. Most exchange groups share the philosophy of the Rev. Charles Filson, founder of the Illinois Multiple Listing Service: "Doing together what no one agency can do alone."

While such exchanges generally list "hard-to-place" children, what is difficult for one agency in one community may be routine for another agency elsewhere. A Mexican-American child may be hard to place in California but not in Iowa. A black child from Georgia may be placed more readily in Minnesota. Children may be considered difficult to place because of age, racial background, medical or emotional problems, or because several brothers or sisters must be placed together. There may be no families waiting for such children in the city or town where they are located. But there may be

67

The Adoption Adviser

MONTHLY LISTING OF CHILD REGISTRATIONS WITH
STATE ADOPTION EXCHANGE

June 1975

1. Initials B.R. (m)   Exchange Reg. No. 201234 Agency Code No. 104
Date of Birth 5/30/66 Religion Catholic   Ethnic Bkgd. Bl./
                                                      Puerto Rican
Personality and Adjustment   He is a hyperactive child who does not
adjust well to change because of insecurity. At times destructive. Needs
stability and firmness to overcome this behavior.
Health   minimal brain dysfunction with perceptual problems.
Agency Plan: ☒ Ready for Placement   ☐ Temporarily not placeable
             ☐ Permanently not placeable

2. Initials A.M. (m)   Exchange Reg. No. 201235 Agency code No. 107
Date of Birth 7/23/67 Religion Protestant   Ethnic Bkgd. Black
Personality and Adjustment   A shy child doing average work in the
second grade. Good adjustment in the foster home. Should be placed with
his brother.
Health   no health problems.
Agency Plan: ☒ Ready for Placement   ☐ Temporarily not placeable
             ☐ Permanently not placeable

3. Initials D.M. (m)   Exchange Reg. No. 201236 Agency Code No. 107
Date of Birth 9/11/70 Religion Protestant   Ethnic Bkgd. Black
Personality and Adjustment   A bright but insecure boy. Tends to be
aggressive with peers, but making good progress in present foster home.
Should be placed with his older brother.
Health   mild cardiac condition but no surgery planned.
Agency Plan: ☒ Ready for Placement   ☐ Temporarily not placeable
             ☐ Permanently not placeable

4. Initials T.G. (f)   Exchange Reg. No. 201237 Agency Code No. 123
Date of Birth 3/10/63 Religion no preference Ethnic Bkgd. White
Personality and Adjustment   A deaf child attending special school for the
deaf, she is doing average or above work academically. Normal
adjustment and development. Foster parents plan to adopt.
Health   General good health exclusive of hearing loss.
Agency Plan: ☐ Ready for Placement   ☒ Temporarily not placeable
             ☐ Permanently not placeable

68

plenty of potential parents in the next town, or the next state, or somewhere across the country.

Adoption applicants and adoption agencies from any state can contact these exchanges about any child listed; they will be put in touch with the local agency that has custody of the child. The groups that operate the exchanges, with some exceptions, do not place children themselves. Adoption agencies generally view the exchanges as valuable aids that help their own adoption workers to help prospective adoptive parents. If you do not have an agency, you will have to get one to do a homestudy and to decide, along with the agency that has custody of the child in whom you are interested, if the placement would be a potentially good one. Some agencies are reluctant to study a family that insists on a specific child in advance because it commits the agency to approving or disapproving the applicants on the basis of a single child who the agency may or may not decide is suitable for that family. Other agencies may be more willing to consider you for a homestudy if you can show that there are children available for adoption that they can place with you. And having a specific child in mind may be the one consideration that will get you in the door at these agencies.

Addresses of the major adoption exchanges are listed in the directory to this book. Here are some additional details on some of the more widely used exchanges:

Aid to the Adoption of Special Children (AASK), Oakland, California

AASK was started by a California family, the DeBolts, who have adopted six children with major handicaps. It specializes in facilitating adoptions of "special kids"—children with medical problems or physical handicaps, children of minority background, kids over nine years old, and children who have large numbers of brothers or sisters who must be placed with them. AASK puts out a monthly newsletter that is available to prospective parents and agencies in the United States and Canada as well as other countries.

The Adoption Adviser

The Adoption Resource Exchange of North America (ARENA), New York, New York

ARENA is the most widely used adoption exchange in existence. It lists both adoptive children and prospective adoptive parents from all over the United States and Canada. It specializes in listing children who are considered by their adoption agencies as difficult to place in their own localities. ARENA distributes a monthly newsletter that includes pictures and descriptions of representative children available for adoption, along with current information on the availability of adoptive children in general. ARENA is affiliated with the Child Welfare League of America, one of the leading standard-setters in the adoption field.

The CAP Book, Council of Adoptive Parents, Rochester, New York

The Council of Adoptive Parents' Manual of Waiting Children, known as the CAP Book, was started by a dedicated group of adoptive parents with the support of adoption agencies in the Rochester area. The CAP Book now is funded by the New York State Department of Social Services. Adoption agencies throughout the state register children with the CAP Books; each child's picture is placed in the book with a brief descriptive writeup underneath. Agencies and adoption applicants can contact CAP for further information about any child listed in the current pages, which are periodically distributed to agencies and adoptive parents groups. Although children listed in the CAP Book usually are located in New York State, CAP encourages inquiries from other states as well.

The Holt Book, Holt Children's Service, Eugene, Oregon

Holt, one of the leading international adoption agencies, puts out the Holt Book, sometimes called the Blue Book, which contains pictures and descriptions of children in the agency's custody. The children listed—from Korea, South Vietnam, or other foreign countries—generally are considered difficult to place because of age, racial background, or medical problems, or because there are brothers or sisters who must be adopted together. People who inquire about these children usually must meet the Holt agency's own standards for adoptive applicants in order to have their inquiries seriously considered. Unlike most other groups that maintain adoption exchanges, Holt directly places the children it lists.

Illinois Multiple Listing Service of the Illinois Child Care Association (CCA)

This service puts out an adoption exchange book informally called the Illinois Book or the Adoption Listing Service of CCA. The book includes descriptions and preferences of waiting families (without names or other identifying data). It also contains pictures and descriptions of waiting children. Patterned after the multiple listing services in real estate, the goal is to provide a central source of information both for people who are seeking adoptive children and for agencies looking for homes for children in their care. Although most of the children listed are from Illinois, inquiries are welcomed from other states.

There are similar adoption exchange services in other states. In Massachusetts, for example, the Massachustts Adoption Resource Exchange, commonly known as MARE, distributes a book listing waiting children primarily from that state. The New York City Department of Special Services for Children, a public agency, puts out its Red Book listing only children available for adoption in that city. But at these, and most such exchanges, inquiries from families and agencies in other areas are encouraged.

Sometimes, just by being alert for possible sources of adoptive children in your own community, you just might come across a child an agency might not have considered for you, or

71

a child you might not have considered before. That is what happened to Judy and Karl Simmons, parents of two school-age boys, who had put aside the idea of adopting after being brusquely told by a local agency that "there are no young children available." Several months later Judy saw a local television show that featured hard-to-adopt kids from the very agency that had rebuffed their inquiry. While the show's host chatted with several of the children, the station flashed on the screen a telephone number at the agency to call for information about adopting these children.

One of the children on the program was a four-year-old boy who wore a hearing aid. Judy was so excited about him that she called the agency that very afternoon. The Simmonses could not adopt the little boy because the program had stirred such a response that the agency was able to choose from several families who already had homestudies completed. But, as a result of Judy's inquiry, she and Karl were able to have a homestudy by the agency. Less than a year after the TV broadcast that prompted the inquiry, they welcomed a six-year-old girl, also with a hearing problem, into their home.

The Simmonses originally had asked for a healthy toddler, which they had considered an "older" child. The agency had discouraged the couple without inviting them to consider other children. The television show demonstrated to Judy the types of children who needed homes, and the appeal of one particular child led the Simmonses to think about other children they had not even considered before.

"If I hadn't seen that show," says Judy, "we never would have thought about older or handicapped kids, not seriously anyway. And we never would have had Annie placed with us."

Television and radio shows or newspaper articles about adoption can be potential sources for locating a child. Such shows and articles tend to concentrate on the "hard-to-place" children available. But by showing specific children in need of

72

homes, and by showing what a "hard-to-place" child is really like (not so different from other kids, after all), these shows and articles give prospective adoptive parents a chance to consider adoption in the light of real live kids, not just statistics and stereotypes.

Television programs such as "The Ben Hunter Show" in Los Angeles and "Midday Live" in New York have regularly shown children waiting to be adopted. There are adoption newspaper columns in some cities, such as Ruth Carleton's "A Child Is Waiting" in the Detroit *News*. Such columns usually include pictures of the children described. Since there is no central listing of the programs and columns dealing with adoption, the only way to discover if they exist in your area is to contact local stations and newspapers. If they don't have such programs or columns, you may plant an idea.

What these exchanges, programs, and columns show is that, despite the shortage of adoptable babies, there is no shortage of kids waiting for homes. If you are running into "Sorry, no children" responses from local agencies, you may be able to shortcut the process by checking these outside adoption sources to determine if the children who do need homes also would fit into your family. Like the Simmonses, you may come across children you probably would not have considered before; now you may want to reach out to these children.

If you have been approved by an agency, in many cases your caseworker will locate a child for you within a few months after your homestudy is completed, without your ever becoming involved in the locating process. If there is a delay, as the Barcos found, you may have to do some prodding and searching. Finding a child depends upon your worker being informed and aggressive in the hunt for sources of children. If you can help, you will be shortening your wait for a child.

5

Independent Adoptions

Independent adoptions are private adoptions generally arranged by lawyers, obstetricians, clergymen, or other intermediaries without the services of a licensed adoption agency. In a simplified example, an independent adoption works this way:

A doctor has a pregnant patient who does not wish to keep her baby. The doctor contacts a lawyer who handles private adoptions. The lawyer contacts a couple who have inquired about adopting. If they want the baby, they agree to pay the biological mother's medical expenses and reasonable legal fees and other related costs plus their travel expenses to pick up the child when he or she is born.

This is the so-called "gray market" adoption. It is legal in all states except Connecticut and Delaware, assuming certain requirements are met under varying state laws.

There have been periodic upsurges in independent adoptions. After World War II private adoptions increased as many parents sought to sidestep rigid agency requirements dealing with religious matching, finances, and lifestyle. As agencies began to relax their restrictive standards, the demand for independent adoptions slowed. Private adoptions surged again in the early 1970s as more couples turned to private contacts since infants were harder and harder to obtain from agencies without long waits. But in the past couple of years, that has also changed. Today the wait for an infant through private adoption is five years or more, as long as for an agency adoption. Many lawyers who specialize in private adoptions no longer will accept applications for American-born infants, although some offer the prospect of adopting infants from South America.

The shortage of babies, however, has led to a resurgence of a type of independent adoption that operates on the dark side of the adoption field—"black market" adoptions. In such adoptions, babies are, in effect, sold to the highest bidder, often illegally and without any legal safeguards for the adoptive parents. With many couples desperate, especially for blue-ribbon white infants, black market adoptions are on the upswing with babies bringing prices as high as $35,000 or more, adoption and law enforcement officials say. As a result, some adoption groups are warning parents to steer clear of any private adoptions in the United States.

One of these is the Adoptive Parents Committee, one of the oldest parent groups in the United States, which in the past directed much of its counseling and informational work toward parents considering private adoptions. (Its members include both parents who have adopted privately and those who have adopted through agencies.) The committee has stopped referring prospective parents to lawyers for independent adoptions because "we just can't see them going through the heartbreak of waiting years and years for a private adoption or being sucked into the ugliness of the black market," says one member, who adopted two children through private placements. She adds: "Essentially, the practice of independent adoption as we all knew it is dead or dying. The gray market has closed. All that remains is the black market, and we can't in conscience refer people to something as immoral and dangerous as that."

The Adoptive Parents Committee, other parent groups, and adoption officials say that the private placements outside the black market that are continuing to increase involve international adoptions. "We refer people to orphanages in Thailand and Indonesia and also tell them about white babies in South America," says the committee member. "I suppose you could say that reputable independent adoption has just moved south to South America," she adds. U.S. couples increasingly are seeking children from South America through private placements, which are handled much like private adoptions of American kids. Such placements are discussed in the chapter on international adoptions.

But before you consider private adoption of a child either in the United States or abroad, you should have a basic understanding of how independent adoptions are arranged. You especially ought to have some idea of how to distinguish between gray market and black market adoptions. And of why you should!

The Gray Market

Perhaps the best way to understand how a gray market adoption works is to see how a real one was completed. When Bill and Laura Fried decided to adopt, they were referred by their family doctor to a lawyer who arranged adoptions independently. The lawyer, in turn, worked with another lawyer in Florida who had contacts with unwed mothers there.

When the Frieds had their first appointment with the laywer recommended to them, they briefly discussed their feelings about adoption and their inability to have a biological child. The lawyer was convinced that they both were sincere and mature in their approach to adoption, but he warned them that it could be as long as five years before a healthy white infant could be placed with them for adoption. This was discouraging, but the Frieds decided to work with the lawyer. They placed half of the estimated fees for the services and medical care for the baby and biological mother, about $1,500, in escrow.

Almost two years later the Frieds received a telephone call from the lawyer. He knew of a child, now in a Florida hospital, who was born with a club foot. The couple who had been promised this child for adoption could not accept the handicap. Would the Frieds be interested?

Laura initially said no. But after she talked it over with Bill later in the evening, they decided to call the lawyer back and ask to see the child. The next morning the lawyer showed them biographies of the child's parents, with family names removed, and the Frieds made arrangements to fly to Florida to see the child at the hospital.

Meanwhile, the biological mother in Florida had agreed to a change in parents for her child. She signed a new surrender form stipulating that she was placing her child for adoption with the Frieds. Legally speaking, placement of the child was made by the bio mother, not the lawyers, and it had to be approved by the courts before final adoption.

When the Frieds arrived at the hospital, they arranged to have the child examined by a staff orthopedist, who explained to them the type of surgery needed to correct the condition. Bill had checked with his insurance company before leaving home, and he knew his medical plan would cover such procedures.

Bill and Laura decided they wanted to adopt the baby boy. They signed the necessary papers and brought their new son home the next day. A few weeks later their lawyer filed an adoption petition in their home state, and the Frieds subsequently were visited by a court representative. The court official sat and chatted casually in their living room as she examined various documents relating to the adoption. Laura had housecleaned frantically for days in preparation for the visit, but the court study appeared to be a formality in this case.

The Frieds' lawyer filed an adoption petition asking the court to approve the adoption. The legal proceedings took place about six months later, and the Frieds were issued a new birth certificate for their son, Roy, with their own names typed in the space marked "Parents."

The Frieds' adoption was fairly typical of most private adoptions in the gray market. They contacted a reputable professional, in this case a lawyer, who located a baby and helped arrange the legal details of the surrender and adoption. In the Frieds' case, their lawyer and the court both made an informal type of homestudy. In other cases the adoptive family may undergo an actual homestudy by a caseworker from a government adoption agency in the state where the child is located. And they may go to court in that state. As with agency adoptions, complete legal records are kept with gray market placements.

The main advantage of a gray market adoption until recently was that it was a way to get infants without the years of waiting increasingly being required by agencies. But now that advantage is gone. The wait for infants in private adoptions is as long as for agency adoptions. Some people may prefer private adoptions for other reasons—they want to avoid agency red tape. They don't want an agency prying into their lives. Perhaps they cannot get accepted or approved by an agency. Or maybe they still feel a private contact can find them a baby faster than an agency will. You may feel that a private adoption could offer some advantages. But be sure to weigh these against the potential pitfalls. Pitfalls such as:

• Lack of adequate legal safeguards. For one, there is the problem of the biological mother's legal release of her child for adoption and the possibility that she could withdraw her consent before the child is placed. You probably will have a lawyer to protect your interests. But the laws governing adoptions outside licensed agencies are vague and contradictory in many states. Whether or not you will be protected if you run into legal complications, such as the mother deciding she wants the child back, may depend on the laws in your state and the skill of your lawyer. Private adoptions usually involve little, if any, counseling for the unwed mother involved, and it is possible that a court could find she was unduly pressured to release her child for adoption if she should decide to challenge your adoption later.

The rights of the unwed father also have been recently established by the courts. He must sign a release form or at least be notified that his biological child is being released for adoption. Of course, the legal procedures of adoption agencies are not foolproof either, but agencies are more closely regulated than gray market intermediaries.

• No guarantee of anonymity—either for you or for the biological parents of your adopted child. In cases where the adopted parents are known by the bio mother, the adoptive couple may frequently worry about the possibility that the bio mother will return at some future time and demand to see "her"—"my"—child. In reality, this rarely happens; if it does, there is usually no legal basis for the demand to be honored. But the thought can be disturbing.

• Medical and cost uncertainties. If the child you have contracted to adopt dies, is born with serious birth defects, is mentally retarded, or has some other major physical problem, you still may be responsible for all medical and hospital costs even though you may end up without a child. You usually are not obligated to take personal responsibility for a handicapped child. Even if the baby is born healthy, delivery complications and other medical problems could double or triple the estimated hospital bills that you contracted to pay for the mother and child.

79

The major concern about gray market adoptions in the United States today, however, is that you could lapse unknowingly into the black market. How do you know? The sure way is to follow the dollar signs. In a gray market adoption, you pay the legitimate expenses to arrange the adoption—medical fees for the bio mother and child, legal fees for the placement, plus the cost of your own lawyer. On average this ranged between $1,600 and $3,400 total in 1974. Once the price rises over $5,000—and surely over $10,000—there's a good chance you may be moving into the black market.

The Black Market

At first glance, black market adoptions appear not unlike gray market ones. You contact an intermediary, sometimes a lawyer, and he arranges to place a baby with you if you agree to pay certain costs. The key difference is that such operators are not finding homes for babies in return for reasonable fees, they are selling babies at a profit, which makes it a modern type of slave trade. Indeed, in mid-1974 the Los Angeles County Grand Jury indicted five persons on charges of operating an interstate, black market baby-selling racket in California. Prosecutors alleged the group signed contracts with pregnant women and sold their babies out of state for $10,000 to $15,000 per child.

In such operations, middlemen approach unwed mothers, women visiting abortion clinics, doctors, lawyers, and social workers to offer them large amounts of money if they can provide healthy, white babies for adoption. In an article on rising black market adoptions in the *Christian Science Monitor* in the fall of 1974, reporter Curtis J. Sitomer wrote that some pregnant and unwed college girls said they had been offered cash sums up to $25,000 for their babies. Another source reported that prostitutes are being recruited to produce children "for sale" at black market prices, according to the *Monitor* article.

There are several objections to black market adoptions. One is the moral objection to profiteering in the sale of babies. "The ugly truth is that, to many people, adoptable children are considered a commodity," says Arthur Friedman, past president of the Adoptive Parents Committee. "Unscrupulous practitioners in private adoption attempt to justify the application of the marketplace law of supply and demand. The practices that evolve from this thinking are profiteering and gouging."

Mr. Friedman adds: "If met by complacency, instead of condemnation, we will arrive at the final resting place for independent placements—the auction block. Are we not already approaching the time when the child will go to the highest bidder?"

Moral objections aside, there are practical problems with black market adoptions. To start with, selling babies for profit violates the law in many states. So such sellers are likely to avoid certain legal niceties in arranging placements. They may obtain the release for adoption of the child without the proper consent of the biological parents as mandated by law; they may coerce the mother into releasing the child; and they may forge or alter birth records, adoption records, and placement documents. Any one of these acts can invalidate the release or the final adoption. If so, your custody of the adopted child is threatened.

Another problem, as with some gray market adoptions, is a possible lack of anonymity. With a black market adoption, this can have threatening overtones. It leaves you open to extortion or harassment by unscrupulous individuals who may claim, falsely or not, that the biological parents want your baby back unless you pay protection money. If the adoption is on shaky legal ground, you may feel that you have no choice but to pay.

Stay away from people who offer you a child for the "right" amount of money, people who have babies for sale. Not only are they morally and legally suspect, but they may not even be able to come up with a healthy child for you. Again, the best way to tell when you are crossing into the black market is by the dollar amount involved. Such operators have a way of escalating fees beyond the first estimate, for "unexpected" complications that supposedly arise.

How to Protect Yourself

It is possible for independent adoptions to be made safely and with legal safeguards in most states, at least in the case of gray market adoptions. But to protect your welfare and that of your prospective child, you should be cautious about private placements. Parents who have adopted children through independent contacts make the following recommendations for others who wish to follow the same route without falling into the dangers of the black market:

· Deal only with reputable intermediaries.

The people you trust to locate your child should have impeccable professional and personal references from parents who have worked with them, from adoptive parents groups, and from those within their own field of expertise—other lawyers, doctors, and so forth. Honest intermediaries can be found through the grapevine of adoptive parents. Also check your doctor, lawyer, friends, and relatives. Ask them to make inquiries in their own professional and social circles. Clergymen often know of independent sources for adoption, as do many private social workers and psychologists.

· Hire your own lawyer to represent you.

This is an extra cost, but it will be worth it to have someone you know or someone specifically looking out for your interests to research all the legal aspects of private adoption in your state. This lawyer can protect you from fraudulent practices and legal loopholes. Since many independent placements take place outside the adoptive parents' state of residence, your lawyer also should look into the private adoption laws of the child's state of residence. (Many independent placements take place in Florida, Texas, Arizona, and California.) *Again, note that this is a lawyer in addition to any who may be involved with arranging the adoption for you.*

•   If you contract to pay expenses, make sure you get a specific breakdown of the expenses—hospital bills of the biological mother, delivery fees, legal fees, travel costs, and so on. Make certain the fees to the intermediary are limited to reasonable fees for the type of service rendered and are not for procurement of a child. The average fee for private adoptions in mid-1974 of $1,600 to $3,400 included medical and delivery costs for mother and child (averaging between $700 and $1,400) and legal fees averaging around $500 to $1,000 for each lawyer involved. Costs could rise higher if there are medical or legal complications. And with inflation, prices go up quickly. Your own lawyer and doctor can advise you if the estimated costs seem out of line.

•   Once a child is located for you, get as much information as possible on that child.

Get specific details from the intermediary or the public agency assigned to do a formal or informal homestudy on you about the circumstances of surrender for adoption and any medical problems of the biological parents. Before you sign any documents or take legal possession of the child, have the child's physical condition evaluated by your own doctor, if possible, or by a doctor you choose or have recommended to you from the pediatric staff in the hospital where the baby is located.

As domestic contacts for independent adoptions are becoming scarcer and more costly, and involving greater risk, more parents who feel they must work outside of an agency structure are turning south, and east, to private contacts abroad. How this is done is discussed in the next chapter on international adoptions.

6

International Adoptions

Adoptions of foreign children by Americans started as a trickle after World War II, gained momentum after the Korean War, and swelled into a steady stream during the 1960s and 1970s. Just since 1968 the annual rate of international adoptions in the United States has more than doubled to over 3,000. And the sources of adopted children also have changed dramatically. In 1957 more than 70 percent of all international adoptions in the United States involved children from European countries. Today over 70 percent of such children are from Asian countries. And there are a growing number of adoptions of children from South or Central America.

The types of children available for adoption vary depending on the country and the adoption contacts there. Generally, however, infants still are available from many countries, although not always in great numbers. The wait for children usually is not longer than one to two years, even for infants. For example, infants and toddlers are available after less than a two-year wait from some South American countries. But the waiting time decreases as the age of the adopted child increases. The majority of applicants for international adoptions ask for younger children, and also for girls, so the wait for these children generally will be longer than for older children or boys, handicapped kids, or mixed-race children.

As with adoptions in the United States, you basically have two adoptive routes to choose from in making a foreign adoption: agencies or individuals.

You can adopt through an agency that is licensed to arrange adoptions in specific foreign countries. Most such agencies also are licensed by a state in the United States or province in Canada. The largest of these agencies is the Holt Adoption Program. Some countries, such as Korea, have laws restricting adoptions to licensed agencies. Prior to 1973 agencies were not allowed in South Vietnam. But now the situation is reversed, and private placements are discouraged there. Agencies also arrange adoptions in South America, India, Bangladesh, and other countries. International adoption agencies are listed in the directory to this book.

In addition to the formal adoption programs, some countries allow legal adoptions to be arranged by private individuals. Many of the same problems that exist with private adoptions in the United States can occur with independent adoptions abroad, so you should follow the cautions outlined in the chapter on such adoptions. Indeed, the problems with private placements abroad can be compounded by distance, language, and sometimes by the myth that all Americans are rich. In some countries, however, private contacts are the only outlets for adoptions. Private contacts are at least the rule, rather than the exception, in the following countries: Brazil, Cambodia, Costa Rica, El Salvador, Haiti, Honduras, Indonesia, Laos, Lebanon, Mexico, Nepal, Peru, and Thailand.

The major sources of information about such independent contacts are the Foreign Adoption Center in Boulder, Colorado, and local adoptive parents groups such as OURS and APC. Check the directory for addresses of sources to whom you can write.

Many couples turn to international adoptions after first taking a discouraging look at a U.S. placement. John and Irene Connar, for example, went to a group meeting at a local adoption agency after two years of medical poking and prodding led them to the conclusion that they would not be able to have children biologically. At the agency they heard social workers talk of the shortage of babies. They were told that because of Irene's background as a nurse in a school for handicapped children, the only child they could have placed with them in less than two years would be a retarded child or a child with severe handicaps.

At this point, the Connars were not interested in a handicapped child—they felt they could not feel comfortable with such a child in their first attempt at parenthood. But they did not want to wait years for a youngster, either. They wanted the experience of raising an infant, but they wanted it before they were too old to enjoy it.

The Connars went home from the agency discouraged, and they stayed discouraged until Irene saw an article in a local newspaper about three couples who had each adopted children from Korea. Seeing the picture of a smiling Oriental child, Irene decided that it was the baby that was important to them, not its color or race. John, after some discussion, agreed. So Irene traced the couples mentioned in the article through the telephone directory. She telephoned one couple, took a deep breath, and started off the conversation: "You don't know me, but I saw an article . . ."

The information Irene received led the Connars to an international adoption program and, five months after the homestudy was completed, to their son, Adam Kim Connar, who was all of six months old when he arrived in the United States.

Now, two years later, the Connars also have a five-year-old daughter, Suk Hee Elizabeth, also from Korea. By the time the

87

Connars returned to the agency for a second child, there were waiting lists for babies and toddlers. But having had their "baby experience," John and Irene felt they were ready to bypass the wait for another infant and ask for a school-age child.

John talks about his adopted daughter proudly, with a bit of amazement in his voice:

"Suk Hee's adoption went so much smoother than Adam's, and her adjustment has been faster, too. It's really strange. We thought with an older child we would have a lot more trouble, but she has been just terrific. Maybe it's because she's old enough to understand what it all means, because she wanted so much to belong somewhere."

The Connars' introduction to international adoption came unexpectedly—through a newspaper article. Whatever your reasons for considering international adoptions, there are direct steps you can take to find out what programs, and what children, are available. One good starting point in orienting yourself to the international adoption scene involves the adoptive parents groups, which are listed in the directory. Parents who have adopted children from abroad usually are more than willing to share information with others and to show off their families at social gatherings. Being able to see children who have been adopted and to talk to their parents can help you focus your own feelings about foreign adoptions. Such parents also can give you tips on the best ways to approach international adoption successfully.

The procedures for international agency adoptions and placements via private contacts differ in many respects. First, we will take a look at agency adoptions. But even if you are considering a private placement, be sure to read the section on agency adoptions because many of the requirements are the same for both types of placements.

Adopting Through an Agency

First, take a look at each of the programs listed in the appendix to this book. Check off those that seem to meet some of your needs—they have the type of children you are looking for, they have children of the nationality you wish to consider, they can arrange placements in your state. Then write to three or four of these agencies for further information. Each program can give you the most current data about the types of children they have available. Be sure to ask for this. Even the program's own brochures may be out of date by the time they reach your hands. If there are children available from the program, at some point you will be sent an application.

Meanwhile, you should check the department of public welfare or social services in your state capital to see what laws and regulations your state has governing foreign adoptions. Some states, such as Connecticut, have strict laws on private adoptions. If the international agency you choose is not licensed to do adoptions in your state, even if it is licensed in other states, an adoption it arranges may be considered a private placement. You may have to meet special requirements, switch to another international agency, or have custody of your prospective adopted child transferred to an agency licensed in your state. You may even have to personally go abroad to arrange the adoption. The international agency you deal with probably has had experience arranging similar adoptions in your state before, so contact it directly for information on how such placements are handled.

Before your application is accepted by an international agency, you will be required to undergo a homestudy. Some programs do their own homestudies in certain states. Usually, however, you will be asked to obtain a homestudy from an adoption agency in your area. Most international programs can provide you with a formal letter requesting that an agency do a homestudy for you, with the assurance that they will place a child in your home pending a favorite report from the agency.

Be sure to contact the international programs first, before trying to arrange a homestudy on your own. There may be a waiting list of applicants for the type of child you are seeking. Some agencies will put you on a waiting list before you have a homestudy completed, which means that while you are waiting for the study to be finished you still are moving closer to getting a child. The homestudies usually take two to four months, but there may be a waiting list.

You usually will not be given information on a specific child until the international program receives a copy of your approved homestudy. Occasionally, a parent will be provisionally accepted for a hard-to-place child and will be told about the child pending receipt of the study. Once you are formally accepted as a prospective parent, the international program probably will send a picture and some background information on a child—not to you, but to your local agency. If she approves, your caseworker will pass the picture and data over to you and help you make a decision about the child. Usually the international program will choose a child, based on your homestudy and preferences, close to the type you have requested. If you have doubts, however, discuss your feelings with your caseworker. There may be a valid reason why you may not wish to accept a child. Or it may be just a case of the expectant parent jitters. Your caseworker can help you sort out your emotions. Turning down a child does not necessarily mean you will not be considered for another, but your reasons should be good ones.

If you decide this is the child for you, your caseworker will relay the the news to the international program. Then begin the moments when, like most prospective parents, you probably will begin to feel great anxiety. Will you be able to raise this little child, who in his pictures looks so small and so lost?

And isn't there any way to cut through all this paperwork? Your little girl is waiting in that orphanage. The conflicting feelings of joy and doubt are common to many parents expecting children, through adoption or through childbirth. This waiting period is a good time to get involved with the activities of a parent group, with other parents who can share their experiences with you. You can keep busy reading about child care, adoption, and your child's country of origin. All these constructive activities serve the purpose of helping time pass while you are waiting for your new son or daughter.

After you send a formal acceptance of the prospective child to the international agency, it will send you certain documents you will need for immigration proceedings. It also will request certain documents from you for use in the adoption procedure in the child's home country.

Most countries require that a child be adopted by the prospective parents in the child's own country. A few require that at least one of the new parents be present at the adoption proceeding. Most countries, however, allow the international adoption programs to arrange the adoptions through a lawyer who retains power of attorney for the adoptive parents. This means that a lawyer selected by your program in your child's country will act in your behalf during the adoption hearings, so that you will not have to be physically present. Some countries allow the child to be taken out of the country before the adoption decree is finalized, which can shorten your wait for your child.

Documents that you will need to provide to your international agency so they can be sent to the child's home country for the adoption proceeding include your marriage certificate, birth certificate, any divorce decrees, a financial statement, and your homestudy. The international program will provide a power-of-attorney form. At the same time, you will have to file for an entry visa for your child with the nearest office of the U.S. Immigration and Naturalization Services. Under sec-

91

tion 101(b) of the U.S. Immigration and Naturalization Act, a child adopted by an American citizen, or who will be adopted by an American citizen, may enter the United States with a "preferential" visa. In simpler English, this means your adopted child from abroad does not have to wait in line under the usual quota system that may apply to other citizens of his or her country. Instead, your child may enter the United States on a permanent basis as soon as the proper paperwork with INS and the government abroad has been filed—usually two to four months or less.

Currently, you may file for only two such visas and you must be a married couple, one of whom is an American citizen. Legislation is pending to extend the number of visas and allow single parents to make use of them. The exception to this rule involves more than two visas issued to a family to prevent separation of brothers and sisters. You must show evidence that you meet the adoption requirements of your state of residence, usually through a homestudy or preadoption certificate, unless you plan to legally adopt your child abroad with both of you physically present prior to or during the adoption proceedings.

To be eligible for such a visa, your prospective adopted child must be under fourteen years of age and legally available for adoption and emigration to the United States because he has no known parents or has only one parent who is incapable of caring for him and has irrevocably released him. If either you or your child fails to meet the visa requirements, you may not use this type of preferential status. This applies if you have already used your two preferential visas, as well. You will then have to wait out the quota, live abroad for two years with your child after his adoption, or try to get your child into the country with some other type of preferential visa: medical, vistor's, probationary (allowed in before quota number is called), or through a special act of Congress, which takes at least a year to pass and of which you are allowed only one per family. All these are complicated and time-consuming.

Assuming you are eligible for a preferential visa, you would fill out form I-600, which has the formidable title "Petition to Classify an Orphan as Immediate Relative." The I-600, is filed at the nearest INS office together with the child's birth certificate, the release for adoption and emigration to the United States sent to you by the international program, your marriage certificate, birth certificates, W-2 form, financial statement, and any divorce decrees and naturalization certificate numbers. You will be required to submit two fingerprint forms, which usually can be completed at the INS office or at any local police headquarters or federal office building.

Some INS offices now allow you to file your petition without documentation as soon as you know your child's full (original) name and date of birth. This allows the process to begin while you are waiting for the papers to arrive.

If you are not planning to be present before or during the adoption proceeding in your child's country, you will have to submit to the INS proof from your state of residence that you will be eligible to adopt this child when he or she arrives in the United States. In some states this means a preadoption certificate. Such a certificate is obtained by going to court in your state and having your lawyer file a preadoption petition, which essentially is the same as the document your lawyer will file when you are ready for the child's legal adoption, after his arrival in the United States. You will get a letter from the INS for use in court stating that all requirements for visa issuance have been met except for the preadoption certificate. Immigration officials usually will accept the agency homestudy in lieu of making their own investigation. If they do check, it usually is a brief and formal visit in your living room, looking at documents and perhaps asking a few neighbors and employers about your character.

The INS sends its own public health doctor to examine your child in the country of origin to certify that the child is not mentally retarded or a carrier of tuberculosis or venereal disease, and that the child is actually the child whose documents

INS has, with no medical conditions not previously noted. It also is a safeguard for you that the child you are promised is the child who will come here.

When all the necessary papers and procedures have been approved, usually within five weeks after filing unless unforeseen delays occur in scheduling health exams or court dates, your local INS office will give approval to your visa petition. At your request, the INS will telegraph the U.S. consul in your child's native country, who will then issue the visa within one to ten days. If you do not wish to pay for the telegram, the INS will send its recommendation for visa issuance by mail.

While this paperwork has been going on in the United States, similar arrangements have been going on abroad. After the adoption proceedings (if any) or other details have been finalized, the child is issued a passport and exit visa. In some cases, the U.S. consul refused to issue a U.S. visa until an exit visa from the country of origin was granted to the child, and the child's government refused to issue an exit visa unless U.S. entry visa was issued. Thankfully, such melodrama seldom occurs today and most countries have established procedures that must be followed, agreed upon in advance by the various governments and agencies involved in intercountry adoptions.

Having a passport and visas means your child is ready to leave for your home. Travel is arranged by your intercountry adoption program and an escort is provided. Some programs ask that you provide your own escort or pick up the child yourself, but most have regular travel arrangements. You are responsible for the cost of plane fare, which usually is the standard one-way ticket price for children from your child's country of origin to the nearest big city with an international airport (Los Angeles, New York, Seattle, and Chicago are the most often used ports of entry), plus a small amount toward the price of the escort's ticket. Since escorts generally take more than two children with them on a flight, you are not required to pay the full price of the escort's ticket. Some programs have special escort volunteers or arrangements with airlines so there is no escort fee.

You will be told in advance, but usually not too far in advance, when your child will be arriving. It is best to plan not to be out of town during the month that you expect your child to arrive. If you must be away, arrange for someone to receive phone and mail messages for you, so that you can be contacted if your child arrives unexpectedly.

Overseas flights are notorious for being delayed or cancelled, and often there isn't time to notify all parents of a change in schedule. So before you leave for the airport, call the airline to make sure that the flight is still scheduled for the same time and that your child is still listed as a passenger. Occasionally a cold, stomach ache, or mysterious rash will keep a child off the flight at the last minute.

All those months of waiting and endless paperwork have finally paid off. You are waiting for your child to arrive and are full of a jumble of emotions you can't quite understand. In the crowded airport you can probably spot other expectant parents by the nervous looks on their faces and the teddy bears they carry. Then the plane arrives. After most other passengers disembark, out come the escorts, carrying babies in their arms, holding older children by the hand. They are all so small, smaller than you expected. Some are crying, others are asleep, most look frightened.

Could that be your child? It's hard to tell with those brand-new haircuts and clothes. That's her, the last one off the plane! You reach out your arms and hold your child for the first time. Hello there, I'm your new mommy. I'm your new daddy.

Private Adoptions

With a private adoption of a child from abroad, your initial contact may be a lawyer or some other intermediary in the

95

United States. Or you may make a direct contact abroad with a lawyer, doctor, orphanage director, or concerned individual involved with child welfare, such as a professional or volunteer social worker. Adoptive parents groups often know of contacts, as does the Foreign Adoption Center listed in the directory to this book. Again, consider the precautions suggested for independent adoptions in Chapter Five of this book. For one thing, you should hire your own lawyer to check the private adoption laws in your state. When writing to a private contact abroad to ask for information on children, be sure to ask for personal references.

Even though these contacts may not be licensed agencies, there usually are set procedures to follow. And you still will have to meet the legal requirements of your state and federal immigration requirements. You may also have to find a local adoption agency to do a homestudy for you.

Through a recommended contact, or one you discover on your own, you must locate a child. Usually you must make arrangements for reliable care while the adoption proceedings are taking place. If the child is to remain at an orphanage, you may be responsible for foster care payments. Or you may have to hire a private nursemaid. Even if you are not obligated to pay for the child's care during the period of waiting, you still may want to send vitamins, clothing, toys, or food. If the child is allowed or encouraged to leave the custody of family or orphanage, you might want to find someone willing to take the child in, perhaps a private family. Some good sources of child care contacts are staff members and spouses of the U.S. diplomatic corps, or business and military personnel stationed in the child's country.

If you have not found a recommended lawyer in the child's country, such sources may be able to help you find one. A lawyer familiar with the country's customs, language, and legal framework is essential to help you in the adoption or transfer of custody. If the laws governing children are strict and you do not qualify as an adoptive parent or guardian for the child or there are other restrictions, it is often possible to obtain a waiver or dispensation through application to the proper government authorities. A lawyer also can help you to apply for a passport and exit visa for your child, and to apply to the U.S. consul abroad for an American visa.

An independent adoption is more likely than an agency adoption to require your presence in the child's country. Although you may be saving an agency fee, you could be spending it twice over in plane fare and living expenses while in the child's country. You may have to arrange for an escort or pick up your child yourself. Since there is no agency to guide you, you will have to depend on information from your overseas contacts or from volunteers in the United States who, as members of adoptive parents groups, help other adoptive parents get through the red tape of international adoptions as smoothly as possible. You or your lawyer may have to arrange such details as a visa and passports on your own.

Adoptive parents frequently turn to private international adoptions as the most direct route for obtaining a child without a long waiting period. When their adopted son, David, was three years old, Jenny and Andrew Perry decided to adopt a daughter. They returned to the same U.S. agency that had placed David with them, only to be told that no applications for babies were being accepted. The Perrys felt it was important that their second child be younger than David, so they started to scout around for other sources of young children. A local parents group gave them information about overseas adoption, and friends told them about lawyers who arranged adoptions privately.

Deciding that South American adoptions seemed to be fastest, the Perrys obtained an application from an orphanage in Colombia. They returned the application and the proper documents to the orphanage, and then they waited. Jenny was beginning to feel that their papers must have been lost in the mail, or that they had been rejected as adoptive parents, when finally a letter came, thick with Colombian stamps, four months after they had written.

The Perrys were approved as parents. What's more, an infant girl, born only two weeks before the letter was sent, was being offered to them. The Perrys were to send a copy of their homestudy to the orphanage and pick up their daughter within a month.

Jenny was elated. But as she started to telephone her husband at work, she suddenly realized, with a sense of panic, that they would have to get a homestudy immediately if they were to pick up their daughter within a month. She called another couple who had adopted from the same orphanage and was assured that her agency probably would update the study already done for the adoption of David. Jenny had told their agency about the possibility of adopting a Colombian child, but neither the worker nor the Perrys had felt pressured to update the study because there had been no word from the orphanage.

Fortunately for the Perrys, they were able to get their homestudy updated quickly by a sympathetic caseworker. But they realized that this could have been done during their wait to hear from the orphanage, saving them the anxiety.

The Perrys sent the agency's report of approval back to the orphanage and in return received a birth certificate and adoption release (with translations in English) to be filed with immigration officials. During the two weeks before their departure to Colombia, they got immunizations, passports, a Colombian tourist card, airline tickets, and more and more nervous and excited.

With David left waiting for his new baby sister at his grandmother's, the Perrys flew to Colombia to see their daughter for the first time. During the ten days they stayed in Colombia, tney had their new daughter examined by a doctor there, hired a lawyer recommended by the orphanage to file the Colombian adoption papers, and got an American visa issued for their daughter, Lisa Maria Perry, within one day because they previously had obtained approval from their local INS office in the United States.

The Perrys' expenses totaled about $1,500, which, as Andrew is quick to point out, probably is less than most tourists spend on their South American vacations. For the Perrys, "it was a vacation with a special bonus," Jenny beams.

The waiting lists for infants in South America have since grown much, much longer. But for many people, South American adoptions still are the fastest adoption route for younger children. Some adoption programs have been established in Colombia and Guatemala so that parents do not have to fly there to complete the legal details and to bring their children home. Instead, they can have an escort bring their children to the United States.

After Your Child Arrives

Whether you met your child for the first time at the airport or brought your child home hourself on an airplane, all the hoopla connected with his or her arrival in a new country can be very confusing after a long and tiring plane ride. If your child is old enough to talk, she probably does not speak English. Even if adoption has been explained carefully to her before she left her native country, she still may not completely understand what is going on. It is a good idea to go straight home from the airport and limit visitors for the first day or so. Your new son or daughter has a lot to get used to all at once.

You should, however, get your child to your family doctor or pediatrician immediately, within twenty-four hours of arrival in the United States. Even children in excellent health

99

can have a reaction to the strange new food and water. Diarrhea, stomach aches, and vomiting are not unusual, but they should be treated promptly. Your doctor can prescribe the proper treatment and can make sure there are not more serious conditions, such as parasites, lice, general infections, or pneumonia. A list of health precautions can be obtained from your adoption program or through other parents or doctors experienced with children from abroad.

After your child's arrival in the United States, you will be responsible for registering him or her with the INS every January as a resident alien. Two years after legal adoption, your child will be eligible for citizenship, under a special regulation for adopted children that waives the normal five-year wait for citizenship. How you file for legal adoption depends on the laws in your state, and on whether or not your child was placed by an agency licensed in your state.

Usually, after your child arrives, your lawyer will present a petition for adoption together with certain other documents (birth certificates, marriage license, and so on) to the court that has jurisdiction over adoptions in your community. Most states require a trial period after the filing, usually six months, during which you are supposed to be supervised by a court-appointed representative or the local adoption agency. Some states require a supervisory period before the filing. In either case, this gives time for some regulatory agency to evaluate the progress of the adoption, although in practice such evaluation often is cursory.

The adoption petition is really the only step of the international adoption process that requires an American lawyer, except for preadoption hearings in states that require them. Some people prefer to retain a lawyer to make contacts abroad or fill out immigration forms, but this is not legally required. Immigration forms are now quite simple to fill out and can be done by any person who can read or write. If there are any immigration or legal complications, most lawyers would not be familiar with adoption laws overseas anyway. Parent groups are probably more experienced with immigration problems than any but the most experienced international law consultants. But it is recommended that you hire a lawyer, familiar with adoption laws in your state, to protect your interests in a private placement.

The legal work that must be done for an adoption is quite minimal in most cases. Across the country, most adoption groups say a fee of less than $300 is fair for the filing of a normal adoption petition. In addition to these legal fees, you will have legal fees in the country of your child's origin. If you work through an agency, these are usually included in the fee charged by the agency to arrange the adoption. Some agencies have no other fees, or will waive them and the legal fees under certain conditions, such as the adoption of hard-to-place children by low-income families. Check the directory for specific information on the total expenses of overseas adoption through the various programs. Also, see Chapter Seven on finances.

International adoptions are more complicated than domestic adoptions because everything must be done in duplicate, once in a foreign country and once in the United States. But they do not have to be bogged down in red tape or take longer than a year or two to complete. The majority of international adoptions processed routinely by established adoption programs are completed in well under a year from the selection of a child to his or her arrival in the United States.

With the guidance of a reputable international adoption program and experienced adoptive parents, your adoption of a child from overseas should be a relatively smooth operation. With proper safeguards, a private adoption also can come off without too many snags, though it generally involves much more frustration, effort, and patience on your part than an agency adoption.

101

The worst part, in either case, is the waiting. But even the wait can be beneficial, giving you time to prepare yourself and your family for the challenging and rewarding experience of an international adoption.

7

Adoption and Finances

Adoption used to be almost exclusively the privilege of the affluent—agency financial requirements, high fees, and just the cost of raising a child kept low- and middle-income families away from adoption agencies. Today, the amount you earn is not as important as your ability to manage adequately on that income. Only a very few agencies will require that you have a specific amount of money in savings, or that you own your home. Since the recent decline in the number of children traditionally considered the most adoptable, agencies have put more emphasis on older children and handicapped or minority children who are waiting for homes. And they have switched the emphasis from financial stability to emotional stability as the main criterion for adoptive applicants.

There are various costs in adopting. First, there are agency fees if you go through a private agency, and the legal fees required in all adoptions—fees that can rise for independent placements. There are travel costs for you or your child with an out-of-state adoption or international placement. There may be certain federal tax benefits resulting from your adoption. And more people of average or lower income can afford adoption today because of adoption subsidies, corporate adoption benefits, plus special programs for adoptive children with special medical or psychological needs.

Costs and fees in specific adoptions can vary. Before getting down to specifics, and to get a general idea of what kind of money may be required, and when, consider John and Susan Alverson's international adoption of their daughter, Mary. After the Alversons had applied to an international adoption program in Korea, they were required to obtain a homestudy from a local agency. They paid half the local agency's fee (half was $250) before the homestudy was completed and the other half when the study was finished after about twelve weeks. The fee was based on John Alverson's annual income of $18,000, with adjustments made for certain expenses.

After the homestudy was completed, the Alversons waited and waited for word from the international program. About eleven months later, their caseworker telephoned to report that she had received a picture of an eighteen-month-old girl selected for them. Susan Alverson phoned her husband, and together they went to the agency office that very day to see the picture of their daughter-to-be for the first time. Although they insisted they were sure about this little girl, their caseworker suggested that they think about it overnight. The first thing the next morning, they called the worker to accept the placement, and the formal agreement was mailed to the international agency. So was the first installment of the international agency's fee, or one-third of $650, less a $100 deposit they had paid when they first applied. The second installment was sent four weeks later, and the third after their daughter arrived.

Friends from a local adoptive parents group recommended a lawyer who charged $125 to draw up the needed papers. His fee did not have to be paid until after the adoption was legally finalized in court, which was six months after the child's arrival in the United States. That was a good deal for the Alver-

104

sons because the legal fee usually must be paid in advance of the final adoption. They needed the money, however, because the plane fare for their daughter had to be paid before she would be issued a plane ticket. They paid the $300 fare (for a half-fare, one-way ticket to New York and part of the cost of the escort's ticket) two months after they first saw their daughter's picture and two months before she arrived. The total cost for Mary's "delivery" was $1,575, which coincidentally was about what the Alversons had paid for the hospital delivery of their biological son, Craig, three years before.

The cost of your adoption will depend on the specific circumstances of your case. But the following sections will give you some guidance on what you should expect to pay.

Agency Fees

Agency fees vary widely. Most public, or government, adoption agencies don't charge any fee, while fees may range up to $2,500 at some private agencies. Many agencies now have a sliding scale for fees based on your income and other factors, such as the number of children in your family. Agencies usually will provide specific information on the fee you will be obligated to pay. If you are not told, be sure to ask.

There basically are three types of fee schedules:

1. A token fee, or no fee at all: Again, most public agencies don't charge anything. Some public agencies and some volunteer-run or sectarian programs may charge only an application fee of $25 to $125 for office expenses. Some agencies, both public and private, will waive all or part of regular fees for low-income families or families waiting to adopt hard-to-place children.

2. Set fee: Some agencies charge a standard fee to all applicants. At private and many sectarian agencies, the fees gen-

105

erally range from $100 to $2,500. The average usually is between $300 and $500. For international programs, the international agency's fee can range from zero, but generally from $50 or $100, to over $1,000. The average is $250 to $500.

3. Sliding-scale fee: Many agencies charge a fee based on the adoptive family's ability to pay. These scales can vary from agency to agency. But the following is a fairly typical example of a sliding scale of fees for a private, nonsectarian agency based on a family's income; the agency also would take into account other factors, such as living costs, size of family, and unusual expenses.

SLIDING SCALE FOR FEES

Family Income	Agency Fee
Under $7,000	None
$7,000–$9,000	$150
$10,000–$15,000	$250
$15,000–$18,000	$400
$18,000–$25,000	$500
Over $25,000	$800 (maximum)

For an update of a homestudy that is a year to two and a half years old, this agency charges another $25 to $100. For a study that is over two and a half years old, it charges an additional $75 to $400.

At most agencies, only application fees usually are charged in advance of your homestudy. The rest is due after the study is completed or after placement of a child in your home. If you do not complete your study, you generally are charged only part of the total fee. Many agencies accept installment payments.

106

Legal Fees

When you adopt, you usually will need to hire a lawyer to file the adoption petition with the court after a child has been placed in your home and before the court proceeding to finalize the adoption. Sometimes an agency will pick up the legal fee in cases involving adoptive parents of limited income or hard-to-place children. In most cases, you will have to pay the lawyer, usually before he files the petition with the court. Fees vary, but in most parts of the country they range from $200 to $400 and under normal circumstances should not exceed $500.

Legal fees can soar astronomically with independent adoptions in the gray market. In addition to filing an adoption petition, your local lawyer may have to take other steps to make sure your placement is legal under the laws of your state. As a result, his fee could range from $400 to over $1,000. Also, you may pay fees to an out-of-state attorney who makes the adoption arrangements for fees ranging between $500 and $1,000. Legal fees for black market adoptions would be even higher.

Adoption agencies and adoptive parents groups usually can recommend reputable lawyers who will take care of the final adoption proceedings and other matters for a reasonable fee. They also may know of lawyers who will handle certain types of adoptions, such as adoptions of hard-to-place children, for little or no fee. With an adoption arranged by an agency, the legal work really is quite minimal. In fact, some local courts even allow adoptive parents to represent themselves at adoption proceedings so they can save the cost of a lawyer. Nick and Lynn Porcelli, for example, handled their own legal work when they adopted a third child through their county Department of Social Services. After all, they had been through the whole thing twice. "By the time Eddie, our third adopted child, was placed with us by the county, we felt we knew the ropes better than most lawyers," says Nick Porcelli. "And with three kids to support, we wanted to save ourselves that $350 fee."

So the Porcellis went to the courthouse and looked up the state adoption laws. Sure enough, the law was phrased so that "a person known to the court" rather than only a lawyer could represent the adoptive parents. The court allowed the Porcellis to represent themselves at the final adoption proceedings. ("It was the court clerk, not the judge, who was resistant," Lynn recalls.)

In a routine adoption that has been supervised by a county agency, the main reason the lawyer is in court for the adoption proceedings is to tell the court that the parents are who they claim they are. In the Porcellis' county, the family court now allows parents to represent themselves—but only if they have been before the court previously with another adoption and only if the adoption has been supervised by the county agency. Some courts may be reluctant to allow you to represent yourself, and perhaps with good reason. Some adoptions, especially those not supervised by an agency, can be complicated. If you do not know your way around the legal side of adoption, it probably is better to spend a few dollars and hire a lawyer to make sure that all the legal documents are in order and that there are no legal hitches in your adoption proceeding.

Travel Expenses

Normally, you will have travel expenses only in private or international adoptions. If you adopt a child from an agency in another state, perhaps through one of the adoption exchanges, the agency having custody of the child usually will pay for transportation to the child's new home. But you will have to pay your own expenses if you go to see the child, even if the visit is required by the agency.

108

In private adoptions, you usually will have to pay the travel expenses of the biological mother if she wants to travel to have her baby in a particular area; you also may have to pay her expenses to travel back home. You certainly will have to pay your own expenses to go to pick up the child. In some cases, you also may have to pay the cost for an agency caseworker in the state where the child is located to travel to your home for a homestudy.

If you are adopting a child from overseas, you will be obligated to pay the plane fare from the child's country of origin to your home, or to the nearest international airport. You also may have to pay part of the fare of an escort. Naturally, you must cover your travel expenses and those of the child if you go to a foreign country to pick up your child. With such private international adoptions, you also may be required to stay in the country for a few days to take care of legal details, such as attending formal adoption proceedings. Some such adoptions also include foster care payments for the child during the adoption waiting period.

The Cost of Adoption

What does the cost of adoption add up to? That depends on your own circumstances and the type of adoption. On average, adoption costs break down as follows, as of 1974:

• Public agency adoption: Since public agencies usually have no fee, the cost depends on the legal fees charged by your lawyer. These can range from $50 or $100 up to $1,000, depending on the complexity of your case. But the cost usually averages:

Agency fee	0
Legal fees	$200–$400
Total	$200–$400

109

• Private agency adoption: Agency fees very from zero to $2,500. The average cost is:

Agency fee	$250–$500
Legal fees	$200–$400
Total	$450–$900

• Independent adoption: The following are average legitimate expenses for a typical gray market adoption. There is no ceiling on black market adoptions, which can cost over $30,000. The following figures for independent adoptions do not include such additional expenses as your travel expenses to pick up the child:

Medical fees	$700–$1,400
Legal fees (local attorney)	$400–$1,000
Legal fees (out-of-state attorney)	$500–$1,000
Total	$1,600–$3,400

• International adoption: International agency fees can range from zero to over $1,000. With a private placement abroad, there is no agency fee but there may be additional expenses, such as the cost of airplane tickets to travel to the country to pick up your child and to bring him home. For an international agency adoption, average costs are:

Agency fee	$400–$500
Legal fee	$200–$400
Travel costs*	$250–$400
Total	$850–$1,300

* One-way, half-fare airplane ticket for child under twelve to travel to the United States from country of origin.

To this you would add $250–$500 if you had your homestudy done by a private agency.

Benefits and Subsidies

The cost of adoption may still seem beyond your reach if you are a moderate- or lower-income family or if you plan to adopt a child with special needs, such as a physical condition that requires long-term treatment. But adoption today does not have to be prohibitively expensive, or even expensive at all. In most states there are programs to subsidize adoptions by lower-income families and other programs to provide financial or other aid to parents of children with special physical or psychological needs.

In some cases, the company you work for may cover part of your initial adoption expenses. A growing number of large corporations have begun offering adoption benefits to employees. After all, most companies have hospitalization plans that pay most of the costs when employees have biological children. But the maternity benefits of such plans do not cover adoption expenses. R. C. Johnson and Sons, the furniture polish producer based in Racine, Wisconsin, began its adoption subsidy in 1970, and International Business Machines, the computer company, started a similar program in 1972. Such companies generally offer to defray part of employees' adoption costs up to between $500 and $1,000. At IBM, for example, adoption benefits are designed to parallel previously existing maternity benefits. IBM pays 80 percent of the adoption costs up to $800 per child. This covers such expenses as agency fees, legal fees, temporary foster care, and maternity benefits for the biological mother.

If you work for a large company, it may have a similar program. Or it may consider starting one if you suggest the idea. Check with your company personnel officer or your union.

Some states offer adoption subsidies to help not only lower- or moderate-income families but also more affluent people

111

with large families. Private agencies first began granting adoption subsidies in the 1960s in the form of waived fees, payment of medical bills for the adopted child, or payment of a lump sum to the adoptive parents to help pay for special expenses linked with the adoption. Gradually, officials at public agencies in most states decided that a monthly adoption subsidy would cost the state much less than keeping the same child in foster care. The average annual subsidy is less than $1,000, compared with an estimated cost of more than $40,000 a year to keep a child in a tax-supported institution. The main purpose of the subsidy, of course, is to help place a child in a permanent, loving home. But at the same time the state's budget also can benefit.

In 1965 New York became one of the first states to offer an adoption subsidy. By 1975 more than three-fourths of the other states had begun offering some type of adoption aid. These subsidies can cover medical, legal, or boarding costs, or a combination of the three. They can be long-term or short-term agreements.

Each state that offers an adoption subsidy has its own regulations. Some limit subsidies to families adopting a foster child previously placed in their home. Others set a maximum family income level as the eligibility standard. All the states, however, require that the subsidy be arranged before the adoption is completed in court, and it usually must be arranged jointly by the agency placing the child and the state welfare authorities. Each state also sets a limit on the amount of subsidy. Usually the subsidy for adoption is slightly lower than the foster care payment to which the same family would be entitled for raising the same child as a foster child. And usually state agencies will pay subsidies only for children who are adopted out of their custody, which excludes subsidies for foreign adoptions. The adoptive parents, however, do not have to be residents of a state in order to receive the benefits of its adoption subsidy. So, for example, a family from Maine could be eligible for an adoption subsidy for an adopted child from Colorado.

Adoption subsidies vary by state. Subsidies in New York range from about $100 to $150 a month, depending on location and the child's age. Eligibility for subsidies in New York depends on income and the number of children in the family. The more children, the higher the income limit. For example, a husband and wife with three biological children and one adopted child, a family of six, can earn up to $15,450.99 a year and still be eligible for a subsidy. The 1975 eligibility rate in New York State is as follows:

Number in Family	Family Income Limit
2	$7,512
3	$10,675
4	$13,179
5	$15,451
6	$18,187
7	$19,187
8 and up	Add $1,000 for each additional family member

Information on adoption subsidies in your state probably is available from your agency or from adoptive parents groups. You also can contact your state department of welfare, which is listed in the directory.

If you are considering adopting a child with medical or psychological problems, you should find out about the many state and private programs that can assist you with services or expenses, such as a crippled children's fund or state medical rehabilitation programs. Some states pay medical subsidies for adopted children regardless of the parents' income. But private aid programs for children with special needs are especially helpful where no subsidy is available or when the adopted child is not eligible for a subsidy.

113

Jack and Steffi Kovac, for example, knew they could not obtain a state subsidy when they adopted a six-year-old Korean daughter, Son Hee, who was partially paralyzed as the result of polio. The Kovacs, who had three biological children, previously had adopted a partially crippled son, Chris, from a public agency in their city, and the state had paid part of his medical expenses for surgery, therapy, and braces. But the adoption medical subsidy did not cover international adoptions. The Kovacs, however, were captivated by pictures of this sturdy, stubborn-looking little Korean girl, and they were sure this was a child whose problems they understood.

So, with some aid from the international adoption agency, which waived part of its fee because the Kovacs were adopting a handicapped child, the Kovacs were able to save enough to adopt Son Hee. And while they were not eligible for a medical subsidy for adopted children from their state, they discovered that the state did have a crippled children's program for any child residing in the state, regardless of citizenship. The program covered medical costs for physical therapy and orthopedic braces for crippled children, with payments regulated according to family income. Under the program, the Kovacs were required to pay $20 a month toward their new daughter's medical bills, only a fraction of the total cost.

"We really feel strongly about advising parents to consider kids with special needs," says Jack Kovacs. "With all the resources available, handicapped kids aren't any more expensive to raise than other children. And they have so much to give."

If you adopt a child with special needs, you can find help from various state and private programs—state medical rehabilitation programs, community councils, the March of Dimes, crippled children's funds, community clinics, and programs within public school systems. There also are clubs and service organizations that provide counseling, information, and services for children with physical or mental handicaps. They also may provide help in obtaining kidney ma-

114

chines, wheelchairs, tutors, swimming lessons, psychiatric counseling, and other needed equipment or services. Such groups include the Lions clubs, Rotary clubs, the United Cerebral Palsy Foundation, Mothers of Mongoloids, and the Kidney Foundation.

It may take some effort on your part to find the financial or other services you may need to cope with your adopted child's disability. One major source of information is AASK, Aid to the Adoption of Special Kids. AASK, based in Oakland, California (its address is in the directory) keeps a file of contacts of groups that provide services for children with special needs, and it is compiling a directory of these groups that is scheduled to be available in 1975. Sometimes AASK also can provide financial aid, or other assistance, to adoptive parents on a limited basis, regardless of your location or type of child.

Dorothy Atwood DeBolt, who started AASK with her husband, Robert, says, "There is great joy in raising handicapped children. What people worry about most is money. But that's the least of their worries."

Adds Bob DeBolt: "Medical expenses, and even living expenses in some cases, for special children can be paid for by various social agencies and resources like Easter Seal societies and crippled children's services. It is not that much more expensive to raise a handicapped child. The only real difference is that a handicapped child needs more attention and even more love."

The DeBolts have adopted six children with severe handicaps.

Another source for information on programs to aid children with special needs is the North American Council on Adoptable Children, or NACAC. This is a recently formed coalition of citizen groups concerned with children in need of homes. Like AASK, NACAC tries to keep up-to-date information on hand about state adoption programs and subsidies

115

and other assistance available to your family. NACAC's address is listed in the directory.

Federal Tax Benefits

You probably did not think about it when you considered adoption, but adopting a child can pay some benefits when income tax time rolls around. For one thing, you are adopting another tax deduction. And you can start claiming your adopted child as a dependent as soon as he or she is placed in your home; you do not have to wait until the adoption is formally finalized in court. Here is a summary of the possible federal tax benefits. You can obtain specific information regarding adoption and your state taxes from the office of tax revenue at your state capital. California and Minnesota are two states that allow tax deductions for expenses incurred in adoption.

SUMMARY OF FEDERAL TAX BENEFITS FOR ADOPTIVE PARENTS

Exemptions: Dependents

If your adopted child was placed in your home before December 31 of the year for which you are filing a return, you may consider the child as your dependent and claim a full exemption of $750. (In some states you are allowed to claim exemption only for the number of months the child actually has been in your home before December 31 on state taxes.)

Itemized Deductions

1. Taxes: Your adopted child is counted as a member of your family when figuring sales tax, as long as your child was placed in your home before December 31. (In some states

116

federal airplane transportation tax is deductible on state returns.)

2. Child and dependent care expenses: Certain child care expenses and nursery school costs are now considered allowable deductions as specified in the instructions for form 1040. Again, as long as your child was placed before December 31, you would be eligible as long as the other conditions of eligibility are met.

3. Medical and dental: You may include all medical and dental expenses you incur on behalf of your child. If part of the fee given to an adoption agency for the adoption of your child is for medical expenses, you may deduct the amount specified by the agency.

4. Contributions: Fees paid to adoption agencies, even though those agencies may have tax-exempt status, are not considered charitable contributions and therefore are not deductible. Contributions to an agency or program after fees are paid, however, are considered deductible, whether such contributions are in money or in goods such as clothing, food, medicine, or toys sent to the program or orphanage. Anything donated to an adoptive parents group that is incorporated as a charitable, tax-free corporation, exclusive of a membership fee, also is considered deductible. This can be money, travel expenses to and from meetings, and out-of-pocket expenses for the benefit of the group, for which you have receipts.

Senator Russell Long, Democrat of Louisiana, and other legislators have proposed that Congress pass a law allowing adoptive parents to take part of their adoption expenses as income tax deductions. The legislation failed to come up for a vote in the 93rd Congress, and supporters planned to try again in the new 94th Congress that convened in January 1975. Some states and municipalities already allow similar deductions on state or local taxes.

Financial matters should be of concern to you when you adopt. Before you commit yourself to any one adoption pro-

gram, get the agency or contact to give you a complete estimate of costs and check that with comparable programs.
Remember, though, that many of these costs usually can be
paid in installments over a period of time. Also remember that
special subsidies or services may be available depending on
your income and the type of child you adopt. Most agencies
and lawyers are willing to be flexible about financial arrangements because their concern, like yours, is that a child and a
family find each other.

8

Foster Care

If you decide you are not ready at this time to make the permanent parental commitment of adopting a child, there may be an alternative way for you to experience the pleasures and frustrations of child raising—by becoming a foster parent. Children in foster care are homeless children placed in homes on a temporary basis until a biological parent or a guardian can resume custody, or until such custody is legally terminated, making the child free for adoption. Except for newborn infants, most American children available for adoption are in foster care before they are placed in an adoptive home.

Foster homes are needed for more than 100,000 children in the United States. As a result of changing laws on child custody, an increasing number of such children, as well as over 250,000 children already in foster homes, are being released for adoption. In many cases such children are being adopted by their foster parents. Some states even have begun preadoptive foster home programs in which children are placed in homes with the assumption that they eventually will become free for adoption by the foster parents.

Despite such changes, however, foster care cannot be considered a trial run for adoption. With adoption, you start with the premise that "this is for keeps." But most agencies, including those with liberal programs, caution foster parents to approach foster care without expectations that the foster child will be released for adoption. Taking on a foster child with the primary motivation of adoption, rather than to provide interim shelter and reassurance to a child separated from a family, can lead to confusion and heartbreak for both the foster parents and the child. Although times are changing, under present laws a biological parent often can legally reclaim custody of a foster child despite years of neglect.

In 1973, for example, a Pennsylvania Juvenile Court judge ruled that the Stapleton family had to give up their five-year-old foster son, Brent, who had been in their home since the age of one, and return him to his biological parents. The county child care service, which technically had custody of Brent, supported the bio parents' demands that the child be returned to them. The child's mother had a history of child abuse and mental instability, and the father had a drinking problem. The judge acknowledged that, "If . . . the best interests of the child received paramount consideration, this court could readily determine that young Brent would obtain greater advantages and benefits" with the Stapletons, the only parents he had ever known. But the judge concluded that "the natural parents have natural rights and obligations and are entitled to their child." He added, "The family itself is an institution whose sanctity must be preserved." By "family," the judge meant the biological family. And his decision was upheld by the Pennsylvania Supreme Court.

Many adoption authorities disagree with such interpretations, arguing that the interests of the child should be "paramount" and not the "natural rights" of biological parents. "To safeguard child care agency policy, to enforce a contract, and to preserve a nonexistent family, the court sacrificed the future of a child," says Joseph Goldstein, Walton Hall Professor of Law, Science and Social Policy at Yale University Law School and coauthor of the book *Beyond the Best Interests of the Child*. And some courts are beginning to put more emphasis on the rights of foster children.

Despite such problems, most child welfare officials believe homeless children are far better off in the homes of foster parents than they are in an institution—assuming that the foster parents have a realistic understanding of their role. Officials have recognized that the 1,400 child welfare institutions that house foster children in the United States do not provide the best climate for homeless children to grow in. Children need a substitute family when their own cannot care for them. An institution, no matter how modern or efficiently run, cannot provide the daily and continuing support that a child must have from a parent-figure adult in a home setting.

Many child care officials agree that more programs are needed to help parents who temporarily give up custody of their children—perhaps because of financial or personal problems, the child's medical needs, and so forth—to reach the point where they can resume custody. While a child was separated from the family, the family would be readied for his return. Services made available to help the family become a functioning unit should include health care, employment training, mental health services, day care and homemaker services, as well as referrals to appropriate resources in the community. Some officials suggest that, before a child actually is removed from a family and placed in foster care, the situation should be carefully evaluated to determine if removal can be avoided by immediate use of various available services, such as employment training.

In many cases, however, foster children are for all intents and purposes abandoned by their biological parents, but such parents may never get around to taking the legal steps needed to release their children for adoption.

121

Whatever the reasons why homeless children are homeless, in every part of the United States the need for foster parents is great. Private and public agencies are looking for couples and single adults to care for children who otherwise will remain institutionalized. Agency policies regarding foster parents vary, reflecting each agency's own standards as well as state and local laws. Generally, foster parents must meet requirements and restrictions on age, marital status, employment, religion, number of children already in the family, amount of space in the home, and other factors. Compared with adoption requirements, agencies tend to be stricter on physical and material requirements with foster parents, with less emphasis on the psychological aspects of caring for a child.

Although agencies may encourage foster parents to consider adoption if their foster child is released for placement, most agencies usually expect foster parents to accept the idea that foster care is supposed to be temporary. Unless the relationship turns out to be longer than "temporary," foster care usually does not provide the deep attachments and permanence that adoption does. Because of changing laws on child custody, in the future foster children hopefully will not remain in foster homes for years, as has been the case, without being released for adoption. Most foster children need help only for a limited period of time while their families are helped with a problem situation, such as illness or divorce. Foster homes also are needed for children who come into the care of an agency suddenly—such as the result of an accident that incapacitates the parents—and who need immediate emergency shelter until it is determined what help the child and family should receive.

If you wish to consider becoming a foster parent, your state's department of public welfare, listed in the appendix to this book, may have lists of foster care agencies in your community. These may include children's homes, institutions, or special schools, any of which probably are in need of foster parents. Also contact local adoption agencies and your county division of public welfare, because they often have foster care units. The types of children likely to be available will range from newborn infants to teenagers. Many agencies regularly place new babies with foster mothers for a month or two until they are placed in adoptive homes. As noted in the chapter on children for adoption, many of those in foster homes are older children who previously were not released for adoption and who then are passed over for adoption because of their age.

Foster parents generally receive payments to cover part of the expenses of caring for a foster child. The average foster care payment varies across the country, but it usually is around $100 to $150 a month for each foster child in the home. This is the boarding allowance. It is augmented by allowances for clothing and medical expenses. The payments are considered tax-exempt under federal tax laws and usually are also exempt at the state and local levels. Ask your agency for the particulars concerning finances.

Foster Care and Adoption

While foster care is considered "temporary" and foster parents are not encouraged to plan on adopting their foster children, this part of the foster care picture is changing. For too many children, presumably "temporary" care stretches into years while the children stretch out of childhood and into adolescence and adulthood. Children are lost in the limbo of foster care and too often are shuttled from home to home without any sense of continuity, permanence, or security. Dr. David Fanschel of Columbia University points out that "temporary" foster care is temporary for only one third of the children in foster care—in the first year of foster care, only three of ten children leave foster homes to return to their biological families or to join adoptive families; after that, only one child out of ten leaves foster care.

Judges, legislators, child welfare professionals, and concerned citizens across the country have demanded changes in laws on child custody, which they claim cause irreparable damage to children "dead-ended" in foster care because they cannot be released for adoption. One of the first states to alter the traditional foster care system was New York. In 1972 the New York Legislature passed into law a bill informally known as the "twenty-four-month review bill." Under the law, which was designed to prevent unnecessary long-term foster care, a homeless child's case must be judicially reviewed after the child has been in care for twenty-four months. Unless there are unusual circumstances warranting an extension of foster care for a limited period, the child must either be released for adoption or returned to his original home, if that situation has stabilized. A child's case may be reviewed anytime before twenty-four months, but the twenty-four-month limit is required by law.

This law and similar laws in other states have freed for adoption large numbers of children who previously would not have been available for adoption. As a result, the number of adoptable children in the United States has increased despite the decrease in the number of adoptable babies.

In some areas where foster children are not automatically considered for release for adoption after a certain time period, the courts have moved to protect the rights of foster children. In contrast to the Stapleton case in Pennsylvania, at about the same time in 1973 a court in Washington, D.C., ordered that a nine-year-old girl *not* be returned to her biological mother and that she instead remain in her foster home. In this case the local child care agency supported demands by the girl's biological mother that the child be returned to her although the little girl had been in her foster home for all but the first eight days of her life. Judge Tim Murphy—citing the book *Beyond the Best Interests of the Child* by Anna Freud, Albert J. Solnit, and Professor Goldstein—wrote that it was the child's best interests alone, not those of either the biological or foster parents, that should determine the outcome of such a case.

And Judge Murphy concluded: "The Court finds that the best interests of this child would not be served by removing her from this warm and happy home she has known all her life, from her foster parents whom she calls 'mommy' and 'daddy,' from her four foster brothers and sisters, to place her in an environment where she feels uncomfortable and anxious, to live in a place she does not want to live and with a woman more an acquaintance than a mother." But experts like Professor Goldstein warn that such judgments are no substitute for changes in foster care laws to allow such children to be released for adoption after a reasonable period of time, such as two years.

Michigan and some other states have special programs that focus on placements of the increasing number of children formerly in foster care, many of whom are difficult to place because of age, handicaps, or race. Many such states have foster parents preference laws providing that foster parents have the first opportunity to adopt children in their care. Foster parents in some states also have the right to petition the courts independently for a release for adoption of a foster child after the foster child has been in their home for a specific period of time.

Some agencies have been experimenting with preadoption programs for foster homes through which children are placed in foster homes with the idea that they eventually will be adopted. In Pennsylvania, which until 1975 did not have a foster care subsidy, quasi-adoptions were arranged by placing homeless children in permanent foster homes. The foster home was periodically reviewed by a local social welfare agency and the arrangement was viewed as a "trial adoption."

125

If all worked out, the parents were encouraged to formalize the relationship through adoption.

Some agencies have specialized adoption programs under which they place children in homes even before the children are released for adoption. The agency decides that certain children probably will be freed for adoption without any problems because of the length of time they have been in care or because of the biological parents' home situation. Such children are "good risks," so to speak, and it is fairly certain that they will not return to their biological parents. While the agency is beginning court proceedings to obtain formal releases for adoption, these foster children are placed in "preadoptive" homes with parents who feel they can accept the uncertain status of their prospective adoptive children. Meanwhile, the children receive the security and stability of a loving home even before they are released for adoption. They do not have to wait in a series of foster homes, as they might otherwise, while the courts grind slowly through the bureaucratic processes.

Only a few agencies, mostly in metropolitan areas, have worked with preadoptive placements for very long, but their experiences have demonstrated the merits of such a program. Other agencies have begun to accept the practice and to imitate it with the children in their care.

The major concern about such preadoptive programs in the eyes of some adoption officials is the uncertainty, however limited, that the prospective adoptive child might not be released for adoption. That uncertainty is reduced further in states where children automatically are released if left homeless for a certain amount of time. That was one factor, for example, in the decision by a Catholic agency in an inner city neighborhood in a large U.S. city when it evaluated the situation of Tony, an eight-year-old boy who was blind in one eye, born of an unwed white mother and an unknown black father, and had been cared for in numerous foster homes all his life. Tony's biological mother had never signed the papers to release him for adoption, but neither had she taken on the responsibility of raising him. The only hope seemed to be a new state law to make Tony eligible for release without his mother's consent.

Tony's current foster parents, an elderly couple, were not interested in a long-term commitment to an active eight-year-old. Theirs was the sixth foster home since Tony had left the agency's institution for preschool children at age two.

Tony's caseworker found a couple who had previously adopted a little girl from the agency and had returned to ask for another daughter. When someone asks for a girl, you usually talk about girls. But somehow the caseworker's instinct told her to talk about Tony, and she did. When the couple met Tony, they were intrigued by him. Eventually, they took him home under the agency's preadoptive program.

Tony's new mother talks about the strain of those first months before her "foster" son was released for adoption: "He tried so hard, and that was part of the problem—that and the possibility hanging over our heads that the courts could decide against Tony, that his first mother would contest the case. But we felt strongly that, if she did, we would fight it—we'd made a commitment to Tony, we were going to prove to him that someone finally cared enough to stick by him."

Six months after Tony was placed in their home, his case went to court. His biological mother did not contest the release, and Tony was freed for adoption by his "preadoptive" parents.

"That was the turning point for him—and for us, too, I suppose," says Tony's father. "He took the letter the social worker sent us [reporting that Tony could now be adopted] and put it on the wall. Later he put a copy of the new birth certificate he was issued after the adoption next to it: It made a big difference to him, being 'legal.' "

Foster care should not be viewed as a test run for adoption, something to be tried to help you decide whether or not to adopt. Yes, foster parents do adopt their foster children in some cases, but this usually is fairly certain only when the agency says, as part of a formal program, "It looks as though this child will be released." New laws moving across the country are making it easier for foster parents to adopt foster children in their care who become available for permanent placement. But as yet, unlike adoption, you cannot start with the assumption that a foster child is "for keeps."

Foster Care: A Summary

Groups such as the Organization of Foster Families for Equality and Reform, OFFER, can help you define and protect your obligations and rights in the foster care relationship. Such groups work with foster and adoptive families, child care professionals, and legislators in the quest to improve the future of children in foster care. Some of these groups are listed in the directory to this book. If you have questions or problems regarding foster care, these groups are excellent starting points.

There are plenty of children who need foster parents. A foster parent needs a high degree of sensitivity and flexibility, with a good measure of common sense and warmth tossed in. Foster care can be challenging and rewarding. Helping a child accept the separation from a loved one, preparing a child for return to his original family, dealing with the problems of a troubled past or preparing a child for a new adoptive home, perhaps yours, involve delicate situations where you must be able to help a child make a difficult adjustment in a time of transition.

Your part in your foster child's development can be critical because you, more than any agency social worker or psychologist, will have the greatest opportunity to affect the child's emotional growth on a daily basis. Good foster care is not merely custodial, it can be the turning point for a child in need.

9

Adoption and the Law

Law in the United States is based primarily on English Common Law, which has little legislative tradition concerning adoption except for inheritance. Therefore, most of the laws on adoption in the various states are statutory legislation established after the mid-nineteenth century. This explains the interstate variations in adoption and child welfare legislation.

At first, adoption laws concentrated on a relationship and rights of "ownership," much like a transfer of property from one owner to another. Later the emphasis shifted to protection of children in the adoption proceeding, and certain standards and policies were established by law. These included provisions for judicial review or investigation of the proposed adoptive parents as well as some established regulations for the termination of prior parental custody. On the basis of age, health, religion, residence, and finances, as well as other more subjective restrictions, the investigations must demonstrate that the proposed adoption would be "suitable" or "in the best interests of the child."

The directory has a state chart that outlines some aspects of present adoption laws; you can consult it for specific information. It should be noted, however, that in many cases the presiding judge has the discretion to interpret and rule as he or she sees fit. The following sections outline the major legal requirements and restrictions to which adoptions generally are subject.

Race

Racial restrictions and restrictions on interracial adoptions have been declared unconstitutional by the Supreme Court. But, in practice, state and local judges can still resist approving adoptions because of racial factors. This is particularly true in such states as Texas and Louisiana, which formerly prohibited interracial adoptions by law. In Illinois, the practice of placing black children in white homes has been discontinued by the state agency.

Generally, however, legal prohibitions restricting interracial adoptions have been eased in most states. Before the Supreme Court ruling upholding such placements, adoptions in New Hampshire, Missouri, Ohio, and Washington could be annulled if they were arranged for parents and children belonging to races prohibited from intermarriage by law. Such intermarriage laws were struck down by another Supreme Court decision.

Religion

Religious requirements in adoption are being challenged today, with strong opinions on both sides of the question.

Religious matching of adoptive parents and prospective adoptive children is required when "practical," when "possi-

131

ble," or is to be given "due regard" in several states, including Delaware, New Hampshire, New York, New Jersey, Ohio, Rhode Island, Washington, and Wisconsin. Well over half the 50 states require some "consideration" of religion, which in turn establishes a basis for the judicial determination of religious matching. If this is the sole basis for rejection of a proposed adoption, however, there is a growing basis for a successful appeal to a higher court.

New laws are beginning to be passed, such as those of Massachusetts in 1969, and Maine and Maryland in 1970, that clearly assure that religion is only *one* of the many considerations in adoptive placement, not the single overriding factor.

In New Jersey a refusal to approve an adoption because of the adoptive parents' lack of belief in a conventional religion was reversed by a higher court. The practical ramifications of this decision will be to provide a precedent for freedom of religious (or nonreligious) views for adopting parents. To deny adoption because of the beliefs or lack of them of the adopting parent may even be considered unconstitutional.

Health

Health requirements of state adoption laws generally are designed to help the court establish the health of the child and the health of the prospective parents at the time of adoption. The law, for example, may require a doctor's report on the physical condition of the child and the parents. Restrictions on the adoption of certain children by parents with specific medical conditions, such as diabetes, may not be written into the law, but the state or agency's own policies may determine whether or not the adoption of a particular child by a parent with a handicap or medical condition is in the best interests of the adoptive child.

The courts also want the adoptive parents to be aware of the health condition of the adoptive child. Adoptions generally are not denied because of a child's physical or mental handicap, but the courts like to be certain that the parents understand, and are able to cope with, the limitations of such conditions.

Residence

Most states require that the adoptive parents live in the state where they plan to adopt for a specific period of time, usually six months to a year. While some states, such as Kentucky, restrict interstate adoptions by requiring the adoptive parents to post bond, others merely require that parents of out-of-state children brought into the state for adoption provide certain legal documents, such as the child's birth certificate, from the child's legal state of residence.

In most states, adoptions have reciprocal validity. This means that an adoption contracted in one state is valid and binding in another. In a small number of states, because of complex inheritance laws, adoptions are only valid if they meet that state's specific adoption laws. Check with your state for specific information.

Age and Marital Status

In all states, adoption is for "adults only." Adulthood is defined by the legal age in the particular state, usually eighteen or twenty-one. Legally, adoptive parents are required to be at least ten years older than the prospective child in many states. As a practical matter, most agencies prefer that

133

parents be at least eighteen years older than an adopted child.

If the adult is married and not legally separated, the spouse must agree to the adoption. The law in some states specifies a certain minimum age for single adoptive parents. In Georgia, for example, the minimum is twenty-five years of age. If the adopted child is older—ten, twelve, or fourteen (the ages usually are mentioned in specific state laws)—he or she also must consent to the proposed adoption.

Aside from such specifics, the general procedures for a legal adoption are outlined by state adoption laws. Some aspects of the law may be waived or modified in unusual circumstances, particularly if the adoptive applicant and child are related. And some of the laws have been changing in recent years because of court decisions.

For example, until 1972 agencies were required to obtain a written release for adoption only from the child's biological mother. Then in April 1972 the U.S. Supreme Court ruled in the case of Stanley versus Illinois that the unwed father's consent must be obtained before his biological children are placed in a permanent home, or that he must at least be fully notified of a hearing on the termination of his parental rights. The ruling, which actually did not involve an adoption but a dispute over custody of children in a common-law marriage, has had a great impact on adoptions. Precisely what voice unwed fathers have in releasing children for adoption has not been cleared up by the courts. In some states, courts and agencies require that both parents must consent to the release of a child. Others require only that the father, if he is known, be notified that the biological mother is releasing their child for adoption. If the father can't be found, the agencies generally are required to make an effort to locate him, such as running small notices in the classified advertising sections of local newspapers. If there is no response after a certain period of time, the child is automatically released for adoption.

In an independent adoption, the unwed mother generally

will sign a release document directly releasing the child to the adoptive parents, usually through a lawyer or other intermediary. In most states, the mother's consent is not legally sufficient unless the biological father is notified of the release and given notice of an opportunity to challenge it. In such states, if he does not show up at a custody hearing, his consent is implied. A release for adoption is legal only if it is written on a specified legal form, which usually is notarized and filed in a court in the presence of a representative of the state or county welfare department or some other specified state agency.

If the mother is married but claimed she was single, the consent for adoption may be declared invalid even if her legal husband is not the child's biological father. The mother's legal husband, at the time of the conception, whether he is the father or not, must be located and notified.

If the mother did not follow the proper procedure for consent to release, the adoption may not be approved until she is located and the proper procedures are completed. If neither the mother nor the father can be located, some courts may consider the child to be abandoned after a certain period of time, usually six to twelve months, and grant the adoption on the basis of a judicial termination of parental rights.

In some states, when the parents' consent is not given for the adoption of a homeless child, the release can be obtained by what is known as implied consent. For example, if parents leave a child in foster care for several years without regular contacts or interest in the child's welfare, and with no plan to reinstate parental responsibility, the courts may decide after examination of the case and a hearing that the parents' actions imply abandonment. This may not be actual physical abandonment, perhaps, but it is an emotional one. The courts often have latitude in interpreting a concept such as abandonment in a broad sense. Death, incurable or protracted mental illness, an extended period of imprisonment or life imprisonment, and occasionally divorce or nonsupport of a child also

135

may be considered as reasons for termination of parental rights without consent.

However, only about half the 50 states have provisions for judicial termination of parental rights in such involuntary situations. In the other states, contractual arrangements determine relinquishment of children for adoption. Biological parents or guardians in these states may then have the right to court hearings before the adoption is finalized in an attempt to reclaim their children. In these states, many times the rights and obligations of parents are unclear, as is the status of the child.

The 1970s have marked a changing in attitudes toward the rights of adoptive or foster children versus the custody rights of adults. The child's right of emotional well-being is gaining increasing importance over the rights of adults claiming custody, whether those adults are biological parents, foster parents, adoptive parents, or relatives. In cases of foster care, adoption, and also divorce, the concept of the adult's right to "ownership" has slipped in favor of the child's right to continuous, stable, and permanent care with a loving adult.

In 1973 the book *Beyond the Best Interests of the Child* introduced the concept of the "psychological parent" as the "real" parent. The authors pointed out that decisions in placing children should reflect the child's sense of time, not the adult's. They also recommended that minors should have legal status as legal parties in all court actions, with the right to have a separate lawyer. This far-reaching book already has made an impact on the child welfare scene and has affected court decisions involving children, such as the Washington, D.C., judge's ruling that it was in the best interests of a foster child to remain in her foster home rather than returning to a biological mother she had never known.

The position of the Children's Bureau of the Department of Health, Education and Welfare is that *all* adoptions should be supervised by an official of an authorized agency, such as the

136

state child welfare division, to offer guidance to both adoptive parents and biological parents, and to submit a final study to the court. Additional psychological and psychiatric services should be readily available before the surrender of a child is accepted. Counseling by a trained professional—a social worker, not a lawyer—should be given to the biological parents; if they decide to end the relationship, complete legal services should be given to petition the court at a judicial hearing for a permanent, irrevocable release. At this point, guardianship would rest with the state or an authorized child placement agency until legal adoption.

Currently, consent is absolutely irrevocable, unless fraud or duress can be proved, only in Florida and Illinois. Minnesota is at the other extreme, with consent revocable until the adoption decree, the court order finalizing an adoption, is issued. The other forty-eight states fall between these two extremes in their laws governing consent for release of a child from parental custody.

Some states have tightened their laws on adoption releases in the wake of the controversial "Baby Lenore" case a few years ago. In that case, an unwed mother changed her mind shortly after signing papers surrendering her baby for adoption. But the private agency, Spence-Chapin, had already placed the baby in the adoptive home of the DeMartino family and the agency refused to return the child. The DeMartinos were not informed of all this until they had had custody of Lenore for a year and a half. Just when, and how, the biological mother tried to withdraw her release was a matter of dispute between her and the agency during a court battle. But finally a New York court created a nationwide uproar by ruling that the DeMartinos would have to return a daughter they had loved for over one and a half years. The family fled to Florida, where a more sympathetic court, operating under different laws, awarded the DeMartinos custody of Lenore and granted them a legal adoption. Controversy over the case

137

led to revisions of many state laws, including New York's, to make a mother's consent irrevocable after thirty days. The New York legislation was known as the "Baby Lenore bill."

Before an adoptive child is placed in a home, most states require that the home be investigated to evaluate the "suitability" of the adoption. Sometimes this is done by state welfare agencies. But if an adoption agency licensed in the state where the adoption is taking place is placing the child for adoption, the investigation is in that agency's hands. The agencies must make what can be considered value judgments, prior to placement of the child, based on their own observations and opinions regarding the prospective parents' income, lifestyle, overall personality, and so on. This is what was discussed in Chapter Three, the homestudy. Once the placement is made, the agency and the adoptive parents sign a placement agreement by which the parents, according to one state's form, assume "complete financial responsibility for the child's care with the intention of adopting him." At this point, the child is in custody of the adoptive couple but he or she technically is still in the guardianship of the agency, which can remove the child from the home if it decides this would be in the child's best interests.

The adoption becomes final when the adoptive parents, or their lawyer, file a document known as an adoption petition, a hearing is held before a judge, and the parents are issued an adoption decree. This is where you as the adoptive parents get directly involved in the legal process. The next section outlines the legal steps you will need to take.

The Law and Completing the Adoption

The legal aspects of adoption can be confusing to the layman, and even to the lawyer. Some of the required adoption forms themselves are very simple. But changes in state laws and local interpretations of those laws can make complex statutes seem even more complex. This is why the legal paperwork for most adoptions, private or agency-arranged, are handled by a lawyer. As noted in the chapter on finances, in many jurisdictions a lawyer isn't required, only a person "known to the court," such as a court clerk or other official who can verify the validity of your representations. But most parents seem to feel safer having someone familiar with legal matters handle their adoption.

Basically, adoption is the procedure to establish the relationship of child and parent between two or three people not previously so related. The adoption formally terminates all prior parental rights to the child, if this has not been done by previous legal actions. If you are adopting through an agency, you usually won't have to round up a lawyer until you are well along—until after a child actually has been placed with you. Independent adoptions can be more complicated because of varying state laws regarding such placements. So you may need a lawyer from the beginning. The appendix to this book outlines the policies of the various states concerning privately arranged adoptions.

Once a child is placed in your home, you usually must wait a certain period of time, normally six months or so, before you can begin court proceedings for a final adoption. This often is considered a sort of probationary period, and your agency caseworker may arrange to stop by your home and see how things are going. During this time your adoptive son or daughter is considered your child—you can, for example, claim him or her as a dependent for income tax purposes, and you are responsible for the child's care. But, officially, the adoption is not final until you obtain the court's approval.

At the end of your waiting period, your lawyer will move to arrange court proceedings for the final adoption. To do this, the lawyer files a petition to adopt with the local court. The purpose of the petition is to give the relevant facts concerning the adoption being proposed so the court can rule on its "suitability."

The petition is a legal document that asks formal permission to adopt a particular child. It will include the following information about you and your adoptive child: legal names, residence, dates and places of birth, date of marriage, brief history of how the child came into your custody, and, in some states, the religion and race of the parties. But rejection of a petition on the basis of racial differences has been declared unconstitutional.

The adoptive parents, through their lawyer, also must file additional documents with the court. These include the child's birth certificate, health report, and legal release for adoption. The child's written consent may be requested if the child is over a certain age. Such documents will be provided by the agency if it is an agency adoption.

Other supporting documents also must be filed: a copy of the parents' marriage license and any divorce papers also must accompany the actual petition.

Usually, you can petition for adoption only in your own state of residence. But sometimes you can file in the child's state of residence, if it is different from yours. Except for Montana and New Jersey, citizenship or eligibility for citizenship is not required.

The court in which you file your petition varies from state to state, and sometimes from county to county within a state. There also may be more than one court that handles adoptions. Family, probate, district, orphans, chancery, and juvenile courts are the courts most commonly used in the various states for adoptions. To determine which court handles adoptions in your county, contact the office of your county attorney. Or ask your own attorney.

Your homestudy or a report from a court-appointed representative will be attached to your petition after it is filed with the court. If all the documents are in proper order, a time is set for a hearing before a judge, usually a private and confidential hearing in the judge's chambers. The hearings generally are very informal. You may be in a regular courtroom. The judge, dressed in a black robe, will be seated behind a high desk or a table. You, the adoptive parents, will be seated in the courtroom along with your adoptive child (and your other children) and your lawyer. Your caseworker may be there.

In a typical hearing, if your caseworker is present, he will "take the stand," that is, he actually will testify that your homestudy was completed, that you have been approved, and generally that the agency recommends that the adoption be finalized. In the absence of the worker, parts of the homestudy may be commented upon. Then your lawyer may ask either the husband or the wife to testify and he'll ask a few questions, mainly to verify that you are who you say you are and that you wish to adopt your child. Then the other spouse will testify.

Since the adoption of small children, who are present at the time, is involved, the formal proceedings can have some very informal moments. During the adoption proceedings for one Maryland couple, the husband's testimony was suddenly interrupted when his one-year-old daughter (the adoptee in the case) climbed on his lap to happily exclaim, "Daddy, daddy." When the father completed his testimony and returned to his seat while his wife was being asked to "take the stand," his three-year-old adopted son leaned over and whispered, with a hint of panic in his voice, "Daddy, do I have to take the stand too?"

Another little boy, just adopted, turned around as he and his family were leaving the courtroom and shouted, "Goodbye, old judge!"

The judge may ask you a few questions to make sure you understand what you are getting into. Or he may go into greater detail. But before long it will be all over. Either your petition is granted or it is denied. If your petition is denied, you can appeal the decision to a higher court. In most cases, the decision is made by the judge on the basis of the documentation long before you enter the courtroom.

If the petition is granted, you will be issued a "decree of adoption" stating that your child is legally adopted and permanently yours. A new birth certificate will be issued to your child, with your last name listed as his or her surname and whatever first name you may have chosen for the child back when he or she was first placed in your home. (Prior to placement, at agencies, some children may have been given code names, such as John Jones, to preserve the anonymity of the biological parents names. At other agencies, children retain their original names when placed.) The place of birth usually will be stated as the original place of birth, although occasionally it is changed to the site of the court. Your name is inserted in the space for parents on the birth certificate.

The procedure for children who are not citizens may be slightly different for the issuance of a birth certificate. Some states will not issue a new birth certificate until after the child has been naturalized, which can take place two years after the final adoption. Citizenship status will not affect the granting of the final adoption decree, however. You will be given the legal adoption papers with your child's new name and can use these to prove the change of name and relationship when registering your child for school, claiming insurance benefits, and filing naturalization applications.

The adoption records are filed in the state of adoption, and sometimes also in the state of the child's birth or former residence if it is different. The records are sealed, and they can be opened only by a court order for what the court deems are sufficient reasons.

In most states, an adoption can be annulled by the adoptive parents only if some preexisting condition was represented

142

improperly prior to adoption. Such conditions may include family history of mental illness or grave emotional or physical conditions. Otherwise, the situation in regard to termination of parental rights by adoptive parents is identical to that for biological parents and their children.

An adopted child is considered yours under the law, but unless you name your child in your will and insurance policies, he or she may not be covered by either. Most wills and insurance policies are written in specialized language that refers to dependents as "issue of marriage," "heirs," "born to," or other similar terms. Your adopted child is not an issue of your marriage or born to you, and may therefore be excluded from the benefits a biological child would be entitled to. Even the phrase "child or children" may not be sufficient unless the policy or will clearly states that phrase includes legally adopted children as well.

Specifically naming your adopted children in your will and insurance policies may be the best safeguard, but you will have to make sure that the documents are updated immediately whenever you have an addition to the family. A simpler procedure may be to insert a clause stating that all biological and adopted children are to be considered equally as heirs and beneficiaries.

You also should make sure your health insurance covers medical and hospitalization expenses for your adopted child from the moment you are considered legally responsible for him (which is when he is placed in your home) and before you go to court. Notify your insurance company of your change in dependents *before* your child is placed with you so that, in the event of an illness or accident, the child will be covered immediately. Some insurance companies and health plans will ask for the child's birth certificate and some proof of your intent to adopt, such as a letter from the agency or a copy of the release from an orphanage abroad.

When a child is placed in your home for adoption, the

143

agency that placed him usually retains guardianship and legal responsibility until the final adoption is completed in the courts. This means that you pay for the routine medical bills along with the other day-to-day expenses of the child but that, as the legal guardian, the agency's permission must be obtained for any major medical procedures, operations, or hospitalizations. Often, the agency will give you a form authorizing such actions in advance in case the child should need them.

If care is taken in planning an adoption, the legal aspects do not have to be overwhelming. In most parts of the country today the legal guidelines for placement and final adoption are being updated and clarified to the benefit of all involved. As more legislatures and judges begin to take into account the best interests of the most important party, the child, laws and those empowered to carry them out will reflect a more rational and humane view of adoption and more parents will be able to enter into adoption on a secure basis.

10

Post Adoption

After all the meetings, questions, forms, and waiting—and, eventually, after a court hearing that seems rather anticlimactic—you and your child can settle down to the business of daily living over the years, to the birthday parties, measles, report cards, and other events that are part of childhood and parenthood. How your family deals with the fact that your child is adopted depends in part upon your child, your community, and your own feelings toward adoption.

The First Days

The big day is here at last. It is the day you go to the agency, to the airport, or (if you are making an independent adoption) to the hospital to see your adopted child for the first time. It is an event every bit as exciting as the first time that other parents get a look at their newly born biological children.

The excitement continues when you take your new son or daughter home for the first time. You will want to have the camera ready to record your child's first day with you in pictures. But it is best not to have a lot of friends or relatives in to celebrate the arrival. After all, your child will need some time just to adjust to you and to his or her new home. Even infants need a few days to get used to a new home. For older children, the adjustment to new surroundings and new parents can take longer. There will be plenty of time later to show off your new son or daughter to friends and relatives.

You will want to share your good news, however, perhaps by mailing out announcements. This was not always true. Until the last decade or so, adoption often was viewed as a kind of hush-hush affair. Older books on adoption devoted at least a chapter to advising parents how to break the news that they had adopted a child, thus revealing that they had not been able to conceive a child biologically. Times have changed. Today adoption is a joyous happening and there is no reason to keep it secret. You can even find a few printed baby announcements made especially to announce adoptions. You also can use the usual baby announcements, inserting the date of arrival under the space for date of birth. Or you can make your own announcement, especially if you are adopting an older child for whom the usual baby announcements would not be appropriate. There are special announcements available from parents groups such as OURS and AFW.

You also will want to share the adoption story with your child. One way to do this is to prepare a special book to tell the proud story of how he or she came to be an important part of your family. A memory book is a special way to share with your child the joy that surrounded the adoption experience. It can communicate to your child the important feelings of belonging and of a mutual shared past in your family.

If your child is adopted as an infant or toddler, you can use a commercially available baby book. Along with the standard entries about weight and height at birth, you can add the date of arrival in your home, his or her age on that day, and other memories of the first exciting days. Again, you also can find baby books made especially for adoptive children. If you adopt an older child, such books are somewhat inappropriate. But the past is still important to your child. Many parents like to start their own books for their adopted children, using scrapbooks or picture albums. You may not be able to put down the date of your child's first steps, but you can include pictures and other memorabilia from his or her arrival day, the first day at school, and other events that make up the tapestry of the past.

In looking at these books together, you can talk of how excited and anxious you were for your child's arrival, how you sat in the agency office or at the airport waiting. You can tell your child about how you laughed and cried at the same time because you were so happy. All of the funny-sad stories about how you adjusted to each other, and the colorful details that make the past vivid and important, will tell how you worked to make a family and learned to love each other in a special way that still grows every day. Children cherish stories of themselves and how they are loved. A memory book is one personal, creative, yet simple way to share and explain the adoption story.

There are factors outside your home that you will have to deal with in the days after adoption. People in your neighborhood, and in your community, will react to your adoption. If your child looks physically different from you, particularly if you are of different racial backgrounds, you may get a lot of curious, although usually friendly, comments or questions from acquaintances or even complete strangers. Comments like: "They don't look like you," "Why are they so dark?" or, "What a wonderful thing you are doing."

Such people usually mean well, and some comments can be amusing (such as the person who, not knowing your child is

147

adopted, coos, "Oh, I can see your baby has your eyes"). But they also can be impolite or inappropriate, especially in front of your adoptive child. It is good that people are interested in adoption, and at the right time and place you may even be anxious to answer serious questions about adopting. But your desire to educate the public about the joys and benefits of adoption may be tempered by the inappropriateness of the situation when the question is asked. It is difficult to be polite when someone asks well-meaning but pointed questions about your children in front of them or corners you in the frozen food section at the supermarket. With some of the comments at such times, you have to fight the urge to give a smart retort: "What a wonderful thing you are doing." Answer: "What, buying spinach?" (The stock answer is, "We're the lucky ones.")

People are more relaxed about adoption these days, and some may approach you for information out of simple curiosity or because they actually want to learn more. Naturally, you should be polite. But you are not obligated to give a lecture on adoption while your children are crying and your ice cream is melting. Also, you may feel certain things belong in the privacy of your family, and you are right. It is perfectly appropriate to say, "I don't have time now. Would you like to come to a parents meeting?" Or, "I don't like to discuss my children in public, or in front of them." Your children have ears, they are human beings with worth and dignity even if they are not adults. You don't have to discuss them like pedigreed dogs just because someone stopped you in the street.

When you adopt a foreign-born child, you and your child will have special adjustments to make. Adopted children who may have spent much of their lives in overcrowded orphanages or children's shelters overseas initially may be behind American children their age in both physical and educational development. For example, they often are physically smaller, except for some children of mixed racial background. Although most established adoption programs overseas screen their children for health problems and have programs to upgrade health standards for all the children in their care, adopted children often arrive in the United States in less than the best of health. This can be aggravated by the long plane trip, and by the change in diet the child experiences in the new adoptive home.

Many adoptive children from abroad are disoriented and frightened when they first arrive at their new home. They are faced with a whole new set of experiences: language, food, an array of possessions and machines unfamiliar to a foreign-born child raised in an orphanage. While some children react to this with restrained behavior, other children who have developed a strong sense of survival will throw tantrums and otherwise exhibit a stubborn attitude toward this strange milieu in which they suddenly find themselves.

Parents who adopted foreign-born children used to be advised against sending their children to school, if they were of school age, for the first year so the child could learn to speak English, feel secure in a home, and have no unnecessary challenges to deal with. Many adoption authorities now feel this is not advisable and instead urge parents to do the opposite. They advise parents to place the child in school as soon as he or she has a medical checkup.

There are several reasons for this change in attitude.

First, children learn best from other children. In most areas, unless there is a great deal of prejudice or there are local racial problems, other children in the classroom will go out of their way to welcome and help a new foreign-born child. Indeed, rather than being an outsider, an adopted child from abroad may find herself something of a celebrity. Children who have a lot of contact with other children have been found to adjust faster to their new situation than children who remain isolated within their own home and neighborhood.

Second, the process of relating to a new set of parents and

brothers or sisters can be very stressful. Removing the child from the household for even a few hours each day gives both the family and the adopted child a chance for a psychological breather. Although it may seem that school would add extra pressure for a child newly arrived from abroad, it instead provides the opportunity to learn about the customs and traditions of his or her new culture in a setting with children of the same age, without the concern for parental approval or disapproval.

Questions About Adoption

The first question some adoptive parents still ask is, "Should I tell my child she is adopted?" Adoption authorities today all agree that the answer is a definite "by all means, yes." The easiest way to deal with the fact of adoption is to deal with it truthfully, as an accepted fact of family life. Letting your child grow up with the knowledge that he or she is adopted is not only the most open approach but also the least complicated. To hide the fact of adoption, as was done in past years, or to ignore it until after the "terrible truth" has been told to the child by someone else, is tragic and unfair. It gives adoption a negative connotation that really does not apply. After all, the adoption of your child is a happy occasion.

On the other hand, to overemphasize adoption can be just as bad as ignoring it. The parent who keeps bringing up his or her child's adoption is bound to make others uncomfortable, especially the adoptive child. If you constantly are telling your child she is adopted, you emphasize the differences instead of making adoption seem natural. This can only cause anxieties for the child, open or suppressed. If you make adoption sound too exalted ("You are special because mommy and daddy adopted you"), your adopted child may get an inflated view of his own self-worth. And it can cause resentment among biological brothers and sisters. The fuss made over "special" children can create the new-baby jealousies with a different twist: Four-year-old Allison, tired of the attention lavished on her new three-year-old adopted brother from Korea by every adult who passed by, suddenly demanded, "Look at me. Aren't I cute too?"

Talking frankly to your children about adoption, in a calm, rational manner, is a good way to lay the foundation for open communication in the years to come. Feelings of trust—and a natural acceptance of such things as adoption, sex, and family relations—can be established at an early age.

Eventually, your adopted child will begin asking questions about adoption. Often, these will deal with his biological parents. Your child's first parents, especially if he or she was adopted as an infant, may never have had the chance to be a real mother and father. Your child probably will want to know why they "gave me away." In explaining why to your child, it is important to reinforce the fact that it was not his "fault," or because he was bad or unworthy of love, that he was "given up." On the contrary, you can say that it was because he was lovable that people were concerned about him.

It usually is pure conjecture to say that the biological mother gave the child up for adoption because she loved him so much and knew she could not provide for him. In most cases, the adoptive parent does not know this. But you do know that, somewhere along the way, many people cared enough to see that your child got to you and to your home—where he or she belongs, safe and sound.

Basically, you can tell your adopted child that the man and woman who helped him come into the world just like every other baby (some adopted children are uncertain about whether they were born the same way that nonadopted children are) "couldn't take care of you, probably because of things beyond their control." Depending on the age of your child at the time you discuss the matter, you can fill in as many of the actual details as you wish. Perhaps the biological parents felt they were too young to raise a child, or the first mother felt she could not raise a child alone, and they decided the child would be better off in another home. Perhaps a parent had medical or other problems that made her unable to take care of a child. Even if nothing is known about your older adopted child's first mother or father, something probably is known about the child's circumstances after birth—the foster homes where he was first fed and rocked, the orphanage where he was kept warm and safe, the agency that looked and looked to find the right family for him. All this information can be given in the positive sense that people cared because he is a precious person.

As your adopted child approaches adulthood, you can provide answers to his questions in greater detail based on whatever information has been provided to you. But don't ask for information from the agency or intermediary that you are not willing to share with your child. If you feel you are ready to handle such private information, then you also must be able to discuss it in the future with your adopted child.

Picture books about adoption available in libraries and bookstores can be useful when discussing adoption with younger children. But sometimes they are inappropriate for your particular adoption experiences and sometimes they even are misleading. Books published before the 1970s focused primarily on the infertile couple choosing a "special" baby. Adoptive parents cannot choose a child like a melon in a supermarket. So this is not really an accurate concept to introduce to a child. Adoptive children and parents do not meet because the parents picked out one particular child from among a line of children offered to them. The idea of being chosen also can raise questions in the child's mind. What if the parents chose wrong? If you can be chosen, can you be unchosen?

If infertility is emphasized as the only reason for adoption, it may make adoption sound like a second-best choice— Johnny might not have been adopted if his mommy could have had a baby of her "own." Some of the newer adoption books dealing with infertile couples take a better approach by explaining that when mommy and daddy were unable to conceive, they simply used another equally positive way to have the child they wanted to love.

Many of the older picture books on adoption also are not really appropriate for many of today's adoption experiences regarding the older child, the single parent, families with both bio and adopted kids, and children adopted across racial or national lines. However, some of the more recent adoption books, listed in the appendix to this book, may suit your adoptive family quite well. They tend to approach adoption as the matter-of-fact yet joyful occasion that it is.

These books not only can help adoptive children put adoption into perspective but also can help adoptive parents. Questions and insecurities have to be dealt with and resolved or else satisfactory parent-child relationships become difficult to achieve. One regret that both parents and children sometimes have is that the child was not born of the adoptive parent. This can be acknowledged so that together parents and child share this small sadness. Part of being together is being able to share the good and the bad, the joy and the sadness. Once a fear or sad feeling is out in the open, it can be accepted. For other parents and children, of course, the fact that an adoptive child was not born of his adoptive parents may not be a matter of concern. To them, it just is not important.

In discussing adoption with a child born of unmarried parents, you may be uncertain about exactly what words to use to describe his beginnings. You should be straightforward. But there is no need to tell a child he or she is illegitimate, a term that implies a kind of disgraceful inferiority. An innocent

153

child is not responsible for something that happened before his birth and should not have to carry a repugnant label because of it. You can simply say to your child, "Your first mother (or the lady who gave birth to you) was not married."

You should be forewarned that the day probably will arrive when your child comes in to tell you that a playmate has called him a bastard. It can be a devastating experience for the child and the parent if you are not prepared for the occasion. Actually, the technical definitions of both the words "bastard" and "illegitimate" imply a legal inferiority, meaning children who are not recognized as legal offspring. In the case of your adopted child, the terms thus do not accurately apply because your child is indeed legally yours. As for the connotation of an unwanted child, that will not matter long to an adoptive child who long has been assured that he or she is loved and valued by you as your son or daughter.

Using the appropriate vocabulary concerning adoption is important. The emotional impact of the use of certain phrases can be harmful. The phrase itself may seem innocuous until you take it to its logical conclusion or use its opposite.

For example, in describing your adoptive child's beginnings, it is best to talk of his biological parents or his first parents, not his "real" or "natural" parents. "Real" parents are the ones that count, the ones who care for a child and share with him or her all the pleasant and unpleasant parts of growing up. The opposite of real would be unreal, and the opposite of natural would be unnatural. Parenthood that is achieved through adoption is neither unreal nor unnatural.

Similarly, some people may talk of your adopted children and your "own" children, if you have biological children as well. *All* of your children no doubt are loved and cherished, and all now belong to you as part of your family. To talk of children who came into the family by birth as your "own" implies that those who came to the family by adoption are somehow not your own. Most adoptive families consider their biological children and their adopted children as being all their "own." It is the *way* that the child came into the family that is different, not the child herself. Adoption is a process, like birth, by which a child becomes part of a family and a family part of a child.

Talking about adoption should be within the context of your child's whole educational experience in the same way that you handle questions about sex, family relations, sharing, friends, religion, and other important parts of learning and growing. Questions about such subjects should be handled truthfully and in a manner you, as the parent, feel most comfortable with. The words used may not be as important as the feelings that are imparted along with the facts. Even without fancy explanations, you can communicate your respect and love to your child and the feeling that you as a parent enjoy your child and helping him or her to grow. With warmth and discipline, you are guiding your child to feelings of self-worth. It is because of this firm foundation of trust, established out of love, that your adoptive child will have the emotional strength needed to face the difficult decisions and realities of life.

Children's Questions, by Age

In the normal development of a child, serious questions about life start at about ages three to five. They are endless and quite natural. Three-to-five-year-olds want to know about the things that surround them, and they also want to know the story of themselves. Questions range from "Why does it rain?" to "Where do babies come from?", all motivated by the healthy curiosity of children.

You do not have to—and you should not—answer more than the child asks at a particular time. Explain what you can, factually, and leave the rest for later questions. Your child will return with more questions when the information you have given has been absorbed into his or her working knowledge, or when more is needed to make the information comprehensible.

Sometimes parents feel overanxious and they overwhelm their children by complicating or misinterpreting simple questions. "Where did I come from?" may mean "How was I born?", but it also may mean, "Was I born in New York or Chicago?" It is important to know what is being asked for, to really listen to your child. So often parents project their needs on the child rather than taking the time to "tune in" to the real situation. A young child usually is not so interested in the mechanics of intercourse as he is interested in what he is. A sense of security, a need for love, often is being asked for along with the facts. Feelings of belonging to you, especially for an adopted child, can be strengthened with positive, open responses.

Young children may not understand or accept the concept that sometimes babies are born from one woman and live with another. Song Oak, a five-year-old adopted Korean girl, talks to her friend, Eric, from kindergarten about getting married and having children. She knows, because of family friends who were pregnant, that children are born to mothers. She also knows that some children come into their families through adoption and some, like her, arrive in the United States via airplane. Song Oak tells her little friend, when it comes to having kids, "Let's do some the American way and some the Korean way"—by airplane.

"Yeah," comes the reply from Eric, "you're lucky you got to come the Korean way. I was just born the ordinary way."

Factual information about birth and other subjects often is rejected by children at this age in favor of explanations that better fit within the context of their own experiences. Children therefore may repeat questions for purposes of clarification, or even reassurance, because one of the ways they learn is

156

through repetition. Just when you think you have gotten the story straight for them, your children will hit you with yet another question that is tougher to answer than the others.

At ages four and five, children seem to project what they have learned into their plans for the future. They practice in their games with other children the roles they assume they will take as adults—mommies, daddies, teachers, police officers, or other grownups with specific duties to perform. They talk of marriage, of having babies, of a thousand imitations of the adult actions and opinions they see around them. How an adopted child thinks adults handle and feel about adoption will be reflected in his recreation of the world as he sees it, in the very real world, to him, of "child's play."

The child of school age, ages six, seven, or older, wants specific details about life. He also wants the reasons behind them. At about age seven or eight, children begin applying a growing sense of logic to the task of defining who they are, building up a sense of self. Their world expands through school, friends, and simply the ability to read. Interests expand, too, and they discover what they like and what they don't like. They begin to make personal choices. And although they are more social, the need for privacy increases.

At these ages, some of the younger child's questions about sex and adoption may be repeated because, as she grows older, the child has a different, more sophisticated level of comprehension than when she was three to five years old. The child is developing a genuine sense of self, which will deepen in adolescence. Again, the child is seeking assurances of worth in her questions, assurances that she is loved and belongs. These questions present an opportune time to build an open relationship with your adopted child. When your child asks, "Why am I here?", and you can respond in a way that assures her that she is loved, a trust is established. That trust can last into adolescence, when you will need all the help you can get in dealing with the conflicts and doubts of a teenager.

157

The adolescent needs to establish himself outside the family circle as part of an attempt to reevaluate his place in the world and in his family. It is almost inevitable that turmoil and problems will arise in the transition from childhood to adulthood. The adolescent, while reexamining family relations and values as they apply to him, is clarifying his understandings in the light of his growing knowledge, experience, and maturity. Adolescents ask for support on the one hand and strongly reject it on the other. They confuse and irritate their parents by being adult, then childlike, and then adult again.

With a teenager who is adopted, there may be additional areas of conflict, especially if the child is of a different racial or national background than his adoptive parents. There are some very real areas of need that arise when a child must work out an identity crisis compounded by the fact that his parents may be different in appearance or different in background. Teenagers must establish who they are, including a sense of racial awareness and identity.

The questions of teenagers may not be directed solely at you, the parents. As part of their growing independence and self-reliance, they probably will seek answers in other places, from their friends and from within themselves. But because they still have not completely made the transition to adulthood, because they are still your children, they still need your parental support. At times, this may be difficult to give and at times teenagers will reject it, but merely knowing that parents are there when needed may be all the security a teenager needs to venture forth more confidently.

The questions teens ask help answer their central concerns: What makes me? How does this affect who I am? For teenagers, the focus at times seems to be on their differences—pimples, growing spurts, and other real or imagined differences or faults. At the same time that teenagers draw a sense of identity from being part of a crowd, they try to be individuals, especially in terms of separation from parents. Yet they return to their parents for help in defining their past.

As part of the search for self, questions about background are inevitable. The need to know about parents and grand-parents or racial or national origins comes up in every family. The teenager tries to come to some resolution with all the diverse factors that brought him where he now stands.

For the teenager who was adopted, these factors become more complex and confusing. Limited information, or no in-formation at all, may be available to him or the adoptive par-ents concerning the child's past. This may only serve to further arouse his curiosity about his beginnings. Some adopted chil-dren strongly feel a need to search for biological parents, or at least to try to find out more about them than is readily avail-able. Others have no interest in finding out more than what-ever general information is available. An "unknown" factor about the past cannot be easily incorporated into a sense of self. It helps an adopted child to at least know that it was not because of any lack of acceptability, any fault of his own, that he was released for adoption. Teenagers usually want reassurances, consciously or unconsciously, of their own worth.

Adoption records generally are sealed so that detailed in-formation about biological parents—such as their names— can only be released through the courts if the court decides there is sufficient reason to do so. Some groups of adopted persons are pressing for increased access to adoption records. The Adoptees Liberty Movement Associates, known as ALMA, helps adoptees over age eighteen search for their roots. So do the Tracers Company of America and Orphan Voyage, a group directed by Jean Paton in Cedaredge, Colorado. The OURS parent group has an annual charter flight to Korea for adoptive parents and their children, organized not to search for biological parents but to discover and understand one part of the past as a family.

After Adoption and Beyond

Even after your child is legally yours, uncertainties about adoption may exist. If they persist, perhaps you should consider returning to your agency for more advice. Most agencies will welcome you without judging you, and they may be able to provide counseling at the agency or through some other source. Unfortunately, however, some caseworkers may be uneasy about dealing with postadoption uncertainties. If you do not feel comfortable with your adoption worker, or if you have not developed a trusting relationship that will allow you to be open with your worker, then you should seek professional assistance elsewhere. Before you commit yourself to a particular family guidance counselor, psychologist, or other individual or program, try to determine whether they view adoption in a positive way or whether they are biased by lack of experience or misconceptions. Talking to other adoptive parents may be helpful. They often can put your own concerns into the proper perspective.

Then again, as an adoptive parent you may not run into any more uncertainties than other parents do. Psychiatrist and author Dr. Daniel Casriel feels that adoptive families have quite a high success rate where parents commit themselves to parenthood and share with their children a full range of emotions "from love and pleasure to pain and anger. A healthy feeling is a healthy feeling."

Your adoption experience is unique because you are. As adoptive parents, none of us will feel or do exactly the same things. But all of us will share certain things because of the children we cherish, children who came to us in a special way.

Adoption is the process by which we start or add to a family. And families are involved in the process of raising children to responsible adulthood. That is our focus: children. And through adoption, a child, a very precious resource, is not wasted but becomes cherished, making our lives richer as well.

Directory of
Adoption Resources

A. Adoptive Parent and Citizen Groups

The following is a list of parent and citizen groups concerned with children who wait for permanent loving homes. Because we are a mobile and changing country, new groups form and old ones disappear or merge, and purposes and programs expand or change. The information here is accurate as of the time that this book was printed, as far as could be determined, and came directly from the groups. Groups with newsletters of extended interest are noted (*).

ALABAMA
Adoptive Parent's Association of Alabama
P.O. Box 5166
Huntsville, Alabama 35805

ARIZONA
Arizona Families for Children
c/o Mrs. Richard L. Keefe
P.O. Box 17951
Tucson, Arizona 85710

The Open Door Society of Maricopa County
c/o Mrs. Madeline Gluck
8332 East Rose Lane
Scottsdale, Arizona 85253

ARKANSAS
Adoptive and Foster Parents Association of Arkansas
1319 Sunny Hill Drive
Fayetteville, Arkansas 72701

CALIFORNIA
The California Citizen's Adoption Coalition (CCAC)
250 East Blaine
Riverside, California 92501
(714) 682-5364

The CCAC is a regional unit of the North American Council on Adoptable Children, an alliance of citizen groups throughout the continent. It has more than a dozen member groups participating in joint programs for the benefit of children without permanent homes, in the state of California.

Adoptaides
Panorama Towers
8155 Van Nuys Boulevard
Panorama City, California 91402

This is a nonprofit corporation of volunteers organized for the purpose of helping the San Fernando Valley

Office of the Los Angeles County Department of Adoptions through social activities with parents and children, work with foster and adoptive families and children, discussions, and other events.

Adoptive Family Association, Inc.
P.O. Box 1236
Ontario, California 91762
(714) 983-6801

AFA was organized in 1969 with the help of the San Bernardino County Adoptions Agency. Members hold monthly meetings the third Friday of every month, work on legislation, publish a newsletter, and have various social events to help promote and further adoptions.

Adoptive Parents Association of Los Angeles
13141 Lake Street
Los Angeles, California 90066
(213) 390-6380

APA is concerned with the well-being of adopted and foster children, and has programs, social events, a newsletter, and special committees dealing with legislation and foster care to implement its goals.

Chow, Inc. (Christian Hope for Orphans of the World)
c/o Robert J. McGown
3712 Chamberlain Way
Carmichael, California 95608

CHOW's main thrust is to receive and send material to orphanages in Mexico and Korea, particularly to those of Holt Children's Services. It also has social events, fundraising, and special programs to publicize this work.

Adoptive Parents Association
c/o Roy Hartman
813 University Avenue
Burbank, California 91504

Adoptive Children's Association of Whittier, Inc.
P.O. Box 797
Whittier, California 94508

Adoptive Parent Organization
1062 Grape Street
Sunnyvale, California 94087

Families Adopting Inter-Racially (FAIR)
1885 Everglades Drive
Milpitas, California 95035

Adoptive families who have adopted across racial lines in the Santa Clara County and San Jose area form a support group called FAIR, which has social events, campouts, dialogues and discussions, playgroups for children, and a speakers' bureau.

Humboldt County Council on Adoptable Children (COAC)
1156 Azalea
McKinleyville, California 95521
(707) 839-3189

Through fundraising, social events, educational events, and specific assistance to those concerned with children in need of permanent homes, COAC hopes to encourage maximum community effort to help these children.

League of Adoptive Parent Services
1141 Helen Avenue
Yuba City, California 95991
(916) 673-0867

Prospective and adoptive parents join in the social and informative activities of LAPS, exchanging experi-

164

ences, desires, and goals for their children.

Parents' Adoption League
120 East Ocean Boulevard
Long Beach, California 90802

*Open Door Society of Los Angeles
1054 West 78th Street
Los Angeles, California 90044
(213) 292-0936

Although primarily focused on adoption, this group is open to any interracial family as well as other families with a specific concern for children. Activities include publicity about adoption, legislative thrusts, informational programs, campouts, and other social events.

Open Door Society of Santa Barbara
P.O. Box 602
Summerland, California 93067

This group is composed of adoptive parents who are concerned about children in foster care, homeless children throughout the United States and in Vietnam, and helping agencies in their quest to place children in permanent homes. Members are also concerned with the needs of racially mixed families.

Open Door Society of San Bernadino and Riverside Counties
c/o Linda Dunn
250 East Blaine
Riverside, California 92507

*Orange County Adoptive Parents' Association
P.O. Box 1314
Huntington Beach, California 92647
(714) 839-0897

OCAPA is a family-oriented group of adoptive parents founded in 1968, which has a multiple-purpose goal of helping adoptive parents, helping waiting children, and providing public services, informally and formally, that will help all children grow happy and strong.

Riverside Adoptive Parents Association
1693 Opal Drive
Perris, California 92370

RAPA's goal is to generate a growing concern among adoptive parents, adoption agencies, and the community, and to further the philosophy of adoption through education, service, and social activities.

Vista Del Mar Adoption Guild
c/o Sue Stutz
5469 Katherine Avenue
Van Nuys, California 91401

WINGS
c/o Mrs. Mabel Fouse
1528 South Mayo Street
Compton, California 90221

COLORADO
*Colorado Parents for All Children
P.O. Box 4132
Boulder, Colorado 80303
(303) 499-1450

This group of adoptive parents gives information and support to prospective parents as well as to the general public through speakers, social events, newsletters, and discussions.

Parents for All Children
c/o Mrs. Skip Foseter
355 Balsam
Denver, Colorado 80226

Colorado Adoptive Parents' Association
c/o Mrs. Sam Dalton
1331 West Evans
Denver, Colorado 80223

Lucky Mother's Club
1712 South Pontiac
Denver, Colorado 80222
(303) 757-6911

This group was originally started in 1951 and since that time splinter groups have formed in other parts of the Denver area. The groups have fostered friendships and given better understanding of the problems and joys of adoption.

South Suburban Mothers' Club
c/o Mrs. Art Metting
4541 South Utica
Littleton, Colorado 80120

Foothills Mothers' Club
c/o Mrs. Sandra True
120 Flower
Lakewood, Colorado 80026

North Area Mothers Club
c/o Mrs. Judy Martine
6238 Ingalls Street
Arvada, Colorado 80002

CONNECTICUT
*Open Door Society of Connecticut, Inc.
P.O. Box 2162
Meriden, Connecticut 06450
(203) 347-9151

ODS of Connecticut is a voluntary organization of people dedicated to adoption as a solution for children who wait. Members are from all over the state of Connecticut and engage in special committees work such as parents of black children, legislation, international, and the Connecticut Adoption Resource Exchange. There also are discussions, a newsletter, and social events.

DELAWARE
Friday's Child of Delaware
8 Chadd Road
Newark, Delaware 19711

This group has social exchanges and irregular meetings to discuss mutual problems in raising adoptive children.

DISTRICT OF COLUMBIA
*The Council on Adoptable Children, Inc.
7013 Buxton Terrace
Bethesda, Maryland 20034
(301) 320-3357

One of the major functions of this nonprofit group is actualized in its Information and Referral Service, an informal exchange for agencies and families in the District of Columbia, Maryland, and northern Virginia area. Through various activities, both social and educational, members hope to provide a base of community action, education, and support on behalf of waiting children and the adoptive family. They have also assumed responsibility for federal legislation, reporting to other citizen groups through their monthly newsletter.

FLORIDA
WE KARE
c/o Mr. William Clark
200 Grace Boulevard
Altamont Springs, Florida 32701

166

GEORGIA
CSRA Adoptive Parents Organization
c/o Mrs. Morgan Wheeler
1652 Pendleton Road
Augusta, Georgia 30904

ILLINOIS
Chosen Parents of Illinois
c/o Mr. Herman H. Harden
P.O. Box 7
Raritan, Illinois 61471

Quad City Council on Adoptable
Children
C/o J. E. Bruner
810 54th Street B
Moline, Illinois 61265

Council on Adoptable Children
c/o Samuel Mungo
1501 East Washington
Bloomington, Illinois 61701

Council on Adoptable Children
1002 South Busey
Urbana, Illinois 61801

Open Door Society of Illinois, Inc.
(ODS):

ODS
514 Hackberry Drive
Arlington Heights, Illinois 60004

ODS McHenry County Chapter
c/o Rol Jeske
639 Elsinoor Lane
Crystal Lake, Illinois 60014

ODS
c/o Jack Kerrill
720 Madison Street
Evanston, Illinois 60202

ODS
c/o Jeff Strack
R.R. 2
Sycamore, Illinois 60178

INDIANA
ARC of Indiana (Association for the
Rights of Children)
ARC of South Bend
P.O. Box 2092
South Bend, Indiana 46624

*Indianapolis ARC
25 West 49th Street
Indianapolis, Indiana 46208

Fort Wayne ARC
4323 South Park Drive
Fort Wayne, Indiana

IOWA
Open Door Society of Cedar Rapids-
Iowa City
c/o Jerry Musser
Route 4
Iowa City, Iowa 52240

This parent group is primarily concerned with children considered hard to place and its social and informational support and educational activities are geared in this direction.

*Council on Adoptable Children
254 Village Drive
Ames, Iowa 50010

This group of parents from the Des Moines-Ames area helps parents and agencies concerned with the hard-to-place child and serves a supportive and social role for families who have adopted such children.

Council on Adoptable Children
411 West Clonton
Indianola, Iowa 50125

Sharing Through Adoption Club
841 Hardy
Akron, Ohio 51001

Interested parents and others from Iowa, South Dakota, and Nebraska

167

join in this group to promote adoption and provide fellowship and shared experiences for adoptive families.

HOLTAP of Iowa
c/o Warren Cateron
3220 East Douglas
Des Moines, Iowa 50125

Members of this group have primarily adopted through the Holt Adoption Program or are supportive of its endeavors.

Tri-State Open Door Society
489 South Grandview
Dubuque, Iowa 52001

This group encompasses persons from the tristate area who are concerned with racial harmony and mutual sharing and growth. Members are predominantly adoptive parents.

KANSAS
NCAPO
c/o Rev. Gilbert P. Herman
Catholic Social Service
2546 20th Street
Great Bend, Kansas 67530

Families of Adopted Mixed-Race Children
c/o Mrs. John Boulton
1721 Kentucky
Lawrence, Kansas 66044

Adoptive Mothers' Club
c/o Mrs. Nancee Price
1206 High
Topeka, Kansas 66604

MAINE
*Families for Adoptable Children
P.O. Box 2004
Portland, Maine 04104

FFAC is basically a parent support group doing volunteer counseling and serving as a resource to agencies and parents. Members are involved in various child advocacy programs and try to provide support for legislation in that area.

MARYLAND
Open Door Society of Maryland
P.O. Box 856
Columbia, Maryland 21044

Think Adoption (TAD)
5891 Morningbird Lane
Columbia, Maryland 21045

NCAPO
c/o Morton Friedman
9140 Good Luck Road
Lanham, Maryland 20801

Parents Auxiliary of Maryland Children's Aid Society
3504 Newland Road
Baltimore, Maryland 21218
(301) 243-7688

PAMCAS assists the Children's Aid Society financially and in the offering of services.

MASSACHUSETTS
Northeast Region Adoption Council
c/o MARE
600 Washington Street
Boston, Massachusetts 02111

The region is a unit of the North American Council on Adoptable Children, an alliance of continental citizen groups. More than a dozen groups from the New England states and Canada are working together to benefit children waiting for permanent loving homes.

Adoption Association of Massachusetts
27 School Street
Boston, Massachusetts 02108
(617) 897-9658

AAM is devoted to the legal interests and civil rights of adoptive persons and their families by establishing community, legislative, publicity, educational, and social service programs through local chapters.

*Open Door Society of Masschusetts, Inc.
600 Washington Street
Boston, Massachusetts 02111
(617) 692-2672

ODS provides informal and supportive services to adoptive and foster families and volunteer assistance to several agencies. Ongoing programs involve racial identity and awareness, overseas adoption, family recruitment, and recreational activities.

MICHIGAN
AMKO of Grand Rapids
3710 Cheyenne Drive
Grandville, Michigan 49418
(616) 534-3883

AMKO provides support through recreational and educational activities for families who adopt children through the Holt Adoption Program.

Muskegon Mothers' Group
c/o Henry Dejong
1863 Amity Street
Muskegon, Michigan 49442

Council on Adoptable Children in Michigan:
COAC
c/o Joyce Maisel
19478 Prest
Detroit, Michigan 49235

COAC
1012 Oak Street
Kalamazoo, Michigan 49008

COAC
c/o Barbara Parsons
2125 Clearwater Road
Lansing, Michigan 48917

COAC
20036 15 Mile Road
Mt. Clemons, Michigan 48043

COAC
c/o James Hawley
830 Airport Road
Muskegon, Michigan 49441

COAC
c/o Mrs. John Hoffman
1028 Hoffman Street
Petoskey, Michigan 49770

MINNESOTA
Open Door Society of Minnesota
2230 Como Avenue
St. Paul, Minnesota 55108
(612) 646-6393

The purpose of ODS is to engage in activities that promote the understanding of transracial adoptions and to promote the general well-being of the children of such adoptions.

*Organization for a United Response (OURS)
3148 Humboldt Avenue South
Minneapolis, Minnesota 55408
(612) 827-5709

OURS is probably the largest parent group in the United States, with over a dozen chapters around the state of Minnesota and spilling into Iowa and North Dakota. The majority of the members are adoptive parents of foreign-born children— Thi, Korean, Vietnamese, Canadian, Colombian, Indian and children from other countries. OURS's main thrust is parent education, and in this line it publishes several types of

169

handbooks and other aids, along with an excellent newsletter. It also offers the usual range of parent group activities. OURS is one of several groups (Adoptive Families of Westchester, Friends of Children of Vietnam, and Families for the Future in Scotia, N.Y. are others) who have original note cards available for sale, appropriate for adoption announcements, as stationery, and other uses.

MISSOURI
The Adoptive Mothers' Club
c/o Mrs. Raymond Eifert
P.O. Box 382
Illmo, Missouri 63754

Missouri Open Door Society
(MODS):
Central Missouri MODS
810 Cambridge Drive
Columbia, Missouri 65201

Kansas City MODS
613 West 58th Street
Kansas City, Missouri 64113

Northeast Missouri MODS
222 East Lafayette
Palmyra, Missouri 63461

Southwest Missouri MODS
Route 1, Box 755
Bois D'Arc, Missouri 65612

St. Louis MODS
6199 Waterman
St. Louis, Missouri 63112

West Central Missouri MODS
304 Jones Avenue
Warrensburg, Missouri 64093

Committee on Adoption Reform and Education (CARE)
6401 Wydown Boulevard
St. Louis, Missouri 63105
(314) 725-6079

CARE is a citizen group trying to improve the welfare of dependent children in Missouri through legislation. Although the group is basically an educational committee, there are also social activities.

NEBRASKA
Nebraska Foster and Adoptive Parents Club
1911 South 20th Street
Lincoln, Nebraska 68502
(402) 432-9496

This group hopes to serve as an organ for meaningful discussion between parents and social workers for the benefit of children, to educate the public and parents, and in general to aid the welfare of children.

NEW HAMPSHIRE
Frontiers in Adoption
RFD 4
Concord, New Hampshire
(603) 798-5392

FIA of New Hampshire is an informal group of adoptive parents who share problems and solutions and promote the adoption of the "hard-to-place" child.

NEW JERSEY
Southern New Jersey Adoptive Parents Organization
c/o Mrs. Rosemary Wells
614 South Drive
Atlantic City, New Jersey 08401

Adoptive Mothers Club of Morris County
c/o Mrs. Carole Walters
114 Flanders Netcong Road
Flanders, New Jersey 07836

Adoptive Parents League of New Jersey, Inc.
15 Englewood Lane
Matawan, New Jersey 07747

170

South Jersey Adoption Association
P.O. Box 583
Pleasantville, New Jersey 08232
(609) 645-3124

This group is a loosely knit organization of prospective and adoptive parents seeking to bring children and parents together through adoption and to provide postadoptive support for families.

Frontiers in Adoption
163 Nassau Street
Princeton, New Jersey 08540

Council on Adoptable Children
617 Boulevard
Westfield, New Jersey 07090

*National Council of Adoptive Parents Organization
P.O. Box 543
Teaneck, New Jersey 07666

This group puts out a newsletter called *National Adoptalk* dealing with issues around the country relating to adoption, foster care, and child welfare.

HOLTAP of New Jersey
P.O. Box 234, Old Highway
Whitehouse, New Jersey 08888

The activities of this group center around the adoption of children from the Holt Adoption Program and the support of the Holt Children's Services work.

Concerned Persons for Adoption
16 Fawn Drive
Montville, New Jersey 07045

One of the main functions of this group is to provide support and information for people interested in adopting from overseas. Group members compile and keep current the changing information on international contacts, particularly independent routes. As a service, this information is available to others who send five self-addressed stamped envelopes to the group.

NEW YORK
New York Citizens Coalition for Children
2361 Algonquin Road
Schenectady, New York 12309
(518) 374-7175

This New York State alliance of a dozen adoptive, foster, and citizens groups works primarily on legislation and other programs that affect the well-being of children in care in the state.

Adoptive Parents Committee, Inc.
210 Fifth Avenue
New York, New York 10010
(212) 683-9221

This organization of foster, adoptive, and other parents and concerned citizens has four area chapters: New York City, Long Island, Utica, and Westchester-Rockland.

Council on Adoptable Children of New York City (COAC)
125 East 23rd Street
New York, New York 10010
(212) 677-6830

Council on Adoptable Children-Rockland County
P.O. Box 554
New City, New York 10956
(914) 354-2817

*Council of Adoptive Parents (CAP)
67 Wood Haven Drive
Rochester, New York 14625
(716) 288-7989

171

This active group is involved in many different aspects of adoption: from adoptchats with prospective parents to publication of the CAP Book, to conferences on the older child and racial identity.

Families for All Children Today (FACT)
Box 27
Ouaguaga, New York 13826
(607) 655-1721

Families for the Future, Inc.
P.O. Box 725
Schenectady, New York 12301
(518) 377-8249

Hudson Valley Adoptive Families
40 Biviano
Barket Kennel Road
Pleasant Valley, New York

New York Council of Adoptive Parents
Box 19N
711 Amsterdam Avenue
New York, New York 10025

Open Door Society
5 Standish Place
Smithtown, New York
(516) 265-4396

Parents and Children Together (PACT)
28 Tietjen Avenue
Kingston, New York 12401
(914) 339-4872

*Adoptive Families of Westchester
P.O. Box 127
Dobbs Ferry, New York 10522
(914) 762-4727

This parent group has living room meetings, conferences, and social events for prospective and adoptive parents and also publishes a newsletter, and has available information on older children and stationary appropriate for all occasions, espe cially good as adoption announce ments.

Families for Inter-racial Adoption
100 De Witt Street
Syracuse, New York 13214

Parents for All Children of Chautauqua County
25 Chesnut Street
Westfield, New York 14787

Parents for All Children of Western New York
65 Fancher Avenue
Kenmore, New York 14223

NORTH CAROLINA
Council on Adoptable Children
c/o R. Gwyn
Chapel Hill, North Carolina 27514

OHIO
Open Door of Cincinnati
3809 Ault Park Avenue
Cincinnati, Ohio 45208

The Adoptive Parents Club
1020 Dawnwood Drive
Parma, Ohio 44134

*Council on Adoptable Children of Cleveland
c/o Rob and Rose Lesh
2216 40th Street, N.W.
Canton, Ohio 44709
(216) 492-3604

COAC has several branches in the Cleveland area, all linked by a newsletter and state issues in the field of child welfare, as well as by social and support groups.

*Adopt a Child Today, Inc. (ACT)
19438 Laurel Avenue
Rocky River, Ohio 44116

172

ACT of Ohio is a statewide citizen group working for children's rights. The chapters and affiliates of ACT around the state participate in activities supporting this goal as well as social activities. Chapters: Akron-Kent, Cincinnati, Cleveland, Columbus, Dayton, Ohio Valley, Youngstown-Warren. Affiliates: Toledo, Stubenville, Lorain-Elyria, Painesville.

Project Orphans Abroad
34500 Grovewood Drive
Eastlake, Ohio 44094
(216) 946-3418

POA's main purpose is support for orphanages overseas and parent support and assistance with international adoptions.

OREGON
Open Door for Adoptable Children
4875 Garnet Street
Eugene, Oregon 97405

The main purpose of this group is to dispense information.

Parents for Loving Adoptions Now (PLAN)
Star Route South
Waldport, Oregon
(503) 265-5679

PLAN is involved with multiracial and international adoptions and the needs of special children.

*Portland Open Door Society
c/o Bob Riddle
1736 South East 143rd Street
Portland, Oregon 97233

Open Home Association
c/o Meskimen
4054 North Colonial
Portland, Oregon 97227

MOKY
147 Roundup Drive
Eugene, Oregon 97401

PENNSYLVANIA
Council on Adoptable Children-Greater Philadelphia
P.O. Box 44
Gwynedd, Pennsylvania 18052
(215) 363-1072

Adoptive Parents Group
c/o Dr. Dennis Lebofsky
14021 Faraday Street
Philadelphia, Pennsylvania 19116

Welcome House Adoptive Parents Group
c/o Mrs. Alberta Cohen
R.D. 4, Box 152 A
Quakertown, Pennsylvania 18951

This group is concerned with activities to support the Welcome House adoption program.

Northwestern Pennsylvania Council on Adoptable Children, Inc.
P.O. Box 3461
Erie, Pennsylvania 16508

*Parents of Adopted Children Organization (PACO)
122 West Springetsbury
York, Pennsylvania 17403
(717) 845-2384

The emphasis of this group is on fellowship, education, and recruitment of families for available children. Postadoption support also is a major part of the group's programs. A unique newsletter called *Because We Care So Much* comes from this group, for and by parents with five or more children.

173

RHODE ISLAND
Rhode Island Families for Interracial Adoption
37 Greenwood Drive
Peace Dale, Rhode Island 02983
(401) 783-8246

SOUTH DAKOTA
COAC
c/o Mr. and Mrs. Ken Knutson
Box 168
Colman, South Dakota 57017

TENNESSEE
COAC of Tennessee
c/o Mihal
224 Woodmont
Nashville, Tennessee 37205

TEXAS
*COAC of Texas
P.O. Box 33303
Houston, Texas 77033
(713) 729-3768

UTAH
The Parents of Adopted Orientals of
Utah County
c/o Mrs. Thomas Lamoreaux
American Fork, Utah
(801) 756-6538

VERMONT
*Room for One More
Star Route
Essex Junction, Vermont
(802) 878-4558

VIRGINIA
Council on Adoptable Children
Family Service/Travelers Aid
1309 Granby Street
Norfolk, Virginia 23510
(804) 622-7017

This citizen group supports the
Family Service/Travelers Aid Agency and works in the community to
promote adoption and offer support
to parents.

Friends of the Children's Home Society of Virginia
c/o Mrs. J. R. Williams
311 Clovelly Road
Richmond, Virginia 23221

WASHINGTON
Adoptive Family Association
1004 South 208
Seattle, Washington 98148
(206) 839-8236

Adoptive Parents Group
c/o Mrs. Catherine Donner
Dept. of Social and Health Services
Community Services Division
Bellingham Office L37-1
P.O. Box 639
Bellingham, Washington 98225

Interracial Family Association
3332 Hunter Boulevard South
Seattle, Washington 98144
(206) 722-7862

Washington Association of Christian
Adoptive Parents
4424 Francis North
Seattle, Washington 98103

*Open Door Society
312 North Sherman
Olympia, Washington 98501

Concerned Parents for Adoption
725 West 6th
Port Angeles, Washington 98362

Focus on Adoption Committee
337 Hunter Boulevard South
Seattle, Washington 98144

WISCONSIN
Open Door Society of Milwaukee
610 North Jackson
Milwaukee, Wisconsin 53202
(414) 475-9073

174

ODS is dedicated to fighting for the right of every child to have a permanent psychological home, through legislation, communication, and as an information resource. In addition, members nurture trans-racial families and adoptive families of other "waiting kids."

*Wisconsin Open Door Society
c/o ODS of Milwaukee (above)

WODS is the statewide umbrella for ODS and other groups. *Open Door News*, the newsletter, serves all. Chapters: Northwest Wisconsin (Eau Claire), Fox Valley, Grafton, Waukesha, Sheboygan, Sherman Park, and Madison.

CANADA
The Open Door Society, Inc.
5 Weredale Park
Montreal, Quebec, Canada
331-3823

This is the national headquarters for Canada of ODS, primarily a group committed to transracial adoption.

The Open Door Society, Inc.-Ottawa Branch
1370 Bank Street
Ottawa, Ontario, Canada

La Spadete
1060 Champigny
Duvernay Laval
Quebec, Canada

Families for Children, Inc.
10 Bowling Green
Pointe Claire 720, Quebec
(514) 697-6494 or 697-7296

NACAC: North American Council on Adoptable Children
Temporary address: 250 East Blaine
Riverside, California 92507

NACAC is a newly organized union of citizen adoption groups, and others, across North America, which hopes to benefit waiting children through mutual cooperation on a continent-wide basis. Planned programs include national and international legislation, publicity, informational services, and other projects.

EUROPE
Parent to Parent Information on Adoption Services (PPIAS)
26 Belsize Grove
London N.W. 3, England

International Committee of Adoptive Parents
c/o Dr. Giuseppe Cicorella
Viale Brenta 7
20139 Milan, Italy

SOUTH AUSTRALIA
Integration League of South Australia (ILSA)
48 Green Street
St. Morris, South Australia

The following groups are not citizen adoption groups but they are involved in various ways in adoption. They are included here because of their interest and resources in adoption.

Child Welfare League of America, Inc.
67 Irving Place
New York, New York 10003
(212) 254-7410

The stated purpose of CWLA is "to protect and promote the welfare of children by helping the child welfare agencies and the communities of the United States and Canada provide essential social services for children and their families." It has

175

an influential role in leadership and service in adoption.

CWLA has a variety of activities including the publication of a journal (*Child Welfare*) and a newsletter, and the support of ARENA. ARENA itself, besides the exchange work, distributes a directory of adoptive parents groups and a directory of foster parent associations.

Children's Bureau, Office of Child Development
U.S. Department of Health, Education and Welfare
P.O. Box 1182
Washington, D.C. 20013

The Children's Bureau is the section of the U.S. government concerned with adoption and related areas. It publishes a journal called *Children Today* six times a year. This journal can be obtained for $2 per year from the Superintendent of Documents, Government Printing Office, Washington, D.C. 20402.

NAACP Adoption Project
70 Hunter Street S.W., Suite 205
Atlanta, Georgia 30314
(404) 522-4373

This project involves several social workers working with various adoption and foster care agencies in the Atlanta area to promote adoption of black children by black parents. There is recruiting and organizing of black parents as well.

Adopt Indian Metis Project
2340 Albert Street
Regina, Saskatchewan

Adopt Minorities, Inc.
5314 2nd Street N.W.
Washington, D.C. 20011

Suma, Inc.
2400 Reading Road
Cincinnati, Ohio 45220

Friends of Children of Vietnam
600 Gilpin Street
Denver, Colorado

Besides adoption work and support of orphanages through shipping of supplies and fundraising, FCVN has numerous local chapters around the United States that work on programs and projects. Groups are located in New York, Massachusetts, Georgia, Wisconsin, California, Washington, Illinois, Iowa, Pennsylvania, Texas, and other states. A number of states have more than one chapter.

Committee of 1000
P.O. Box 1390
Highland Park, New Jersey 08904
(201) 828-1382

The Committee of 1000 was initiated because of a concern for children in Vietnam and a desire to establish and maintain a reception center there where children could be treated. Maintenance of the reception center in Saigon is still a major concern but members have also become involved with leper children in Korea and the famine in Ethiopia, among other areas.

Aid to the Adoption of Special Children
Box 11212
Oakland, California 94611
(415) 547-1678

AASK is a nonprofit foundation established to help special kids—older, minority, and handicapped—find permanent homes. AASK acts

176

as a liaison for information about children and families and provides supportive services in the form of financial aid, informal counseling, information, and legal material. Local chapters help the parent organization.

O.F.F.E.R. (Organization of Foster Families For Equality and Reform)
239 Vincent Drive
East Meadow, New York 11554

This organization of citizens is concerned with all aspects of foster care and has worked to support legislation and policy that can keep foster care from becoming a dead end for children.

Columbian-American Friends
308 W. Keech
Ann Arbor, Michigan

Adopt Co-Op
45 W. Pennington, Suite 407
Tucson, Arizona 85701

National Handicapped Parents for Kids
4222 Shenandoah
St. Louis, Missouri 63110

This loosely organized group supports the right of adults who are handicapped to have the opportunity to give of themselves to others, primarily as parents. One of their thrusts is to bring a wider recognition of such adults as potential adoptive parents for non-handicapped children.

Spaulding for Children–New Jersey
321 Elm Street
Westfield, New Jersey 07090
(201) 233-2282

Spaulding for Children–Michigan
3660 Walborus Road
Chelsea, Michigan 48118
(313) 475-2500

LCS-Spaulding for Children
24 West 45th Street
New York, New York 10036
(212) 869-8940

These three adoption agencies, and others like them that are developing in other states, were established primarily through the efforts of adoptive parents, concerned professionals and others involved with the hard-to-place child. They will help agencies place children considered difficult to find an adoptive home for, and help parents considering such a child. Their influence has been great in the placement of children in need of special homes. Spauldings usually charge no fee to the parents.

Another agency that should be mentioned is the adoption services of Tressler-Lutheran Service Associates, York, Pennsylvania, which has one of the most comprehensive systems of services to adoptive parents, particularly in the area of supportive services during the post-placement period.

International Union for Child Welfare
Centre Internationale
Rue de Varembe 1
1211 Geneva 20 Switzerland

IUCW is an international nongovernmental organization for service of children and adolescents. It has consultative status with the United Nations and is affiliated with public and voluntary agencies across the world.

177

Directory of Adoption Resources

American-Korean Foundation
Room 207
345 E. 46th Street
New York, New York 10017

AKF is involved with various social welfare concerns in Korea and also in Vietnam. One of its many programs in Korea is Operation Outreach, aiding Korean lepers and their families. Although AKF itself is not an adoption agency, one part of the Operation Outreach program will be adoption of some of the children, mostly of school age, of these lepers by American families.

PACT (Partners Aiding Children Today)
723 Tenth Avenue South
Minneapolis, Minnesota 55415

PACT is a voluntary organization assisting children abroad, primarily in Vietnam. One of the activities of PACT in the United States is the sponsorship of patients undergoing special medical treatment, such as heart surgery. They have worked closely with the Metropolitan Medical Center Children's Heart Fund in Minneapolis, which aids children from the United States, Vietnam, Korea, Greece, Ethiopia, and other parts of the world. Some of these children were orphaned and subsequently adopted by families in the United States.

United Nations Committee on Adoption and Foster Care
c/o the Honorable A. Brooks
Liberian Delegation to the U.N.
New York, New York.

An informal committee providing consultative services to the U.N.

in the area of adoption and foster care.

Foreign Adoption Resources
P.O. Box 774
Boulder, Colorado 80302

This group provides an annual report, with periodic updates, on information concerning adoption of foreign children for $3.00.

The following groups are concerned in various ways with adolescent and adult adoptees:

ALMA: Adoptees Liberty Movement Associates
P.O. Box 154
Washington Bridge Station
New York, New York 10033

ALMA, which means *soul* in Spanish, was founded by author Florence Fisher to support adopted people who wish to seek out their roots through mutual sharing of experiences and through the fight to change the laws that deny adopted people the right to search for their biological past.

Adoptees Registry
66 Court Street
Brooklyn, New York 11201
(212) 693-7369

Adoption Research Project
P. O. Box 49809
Los Angeles, California 90049

The directors of this project would like to hear from anyone involved with adoptions: biological parents, adoptive parents, adoptees or others, who are willing to share their experiences concerning adoption.

178

Orphan Voyage
c/o Jean Paton
Cedaredge, Colorado 81413

Orphan Voyage was founded by author Jean Paton and aids and guides children "orphaned" by illegitimacy, death, divorce, desertion, or for other reasons. It has helped people in their quest to find parents, siblings, or other relatives and for years has fought against the sealing of adoption records.

B. State and Local Organizations

1. STATE AGENCIES

The following state agencies have listings of licensed adoption agencies within the state or can direct you to the department that currently handles such information. They also can give you information about the existence and functioning of state adoption exchanges and other adoption and foster care services in your state.

ALABAMA
State Department of Pensions and Security
Bureau of Child Welfare
Administrative Building
64 North Union Street
Montgomery, Alabama 36104

ALASKA
Department of Health and Welfare
Division of Public Welfare
Pouch H
Juneau, Alaska 99801

ARIZONA
Department of Public Welfare
State Office Building
Phoenix, Arizona 85007

ARKANSAS
Arkansas State Department of Public Welfare
Arkansas Social Services, Child Welfare Services
P.O. Box 1437
Little Rock, Arkansas 72203

CALIFORNIA
State of California–Health and Welfare Agency
Department of Health
Adoption Services Section
714 and 744 P Street
Sacramento, California 95814

COLORADO
Colorado Department of Social Services

Directory of Adoption Resources

Family and Children's Services
Division of Public Welfare
1575 Sherman Street
Denver, Colorado 80203

CONNECTICUT
Department of Children and Youth
Services
110 Bartholomew Avenue
Hartford, Connecticut 06115

DELAWARE
Department of Health and Social
Services
Division of Social Services
Box 309
Wilmington, Delaware 19899

DISTRICT OF COLUMBIA
Social Services Administration
122 C Street N.W.
Washington, D.C. 20001

FLORIDA
Division of Family Services
P.O. Box 2050
Jacksonville, Florida 32203

GEORGIA
Division for Children and Youth
State Office Building
Capitol Square
Atlanta, Georgia 30334

HAWAII
Family Services
Department of Social Services
P.O. Box 339
Honolulu, Hawaii 96809

IDAHO
Idaho Department of Health and
Welfare
Statehouse
Boise, Idaho 83702

ILLINOIS
Illinois Department of Children and
Family Services
524 South Second Street
Springfield, Illinois 62704

INDIANA
Indiana State Department of Public
Welfare
Division of Social Services–Child
Welfare
100 North Senate Avenue
Indianapolis, Indiana 46204

IOWA
Iowa Department of Social Services
Bureau of Family and Children's
Services
Lucas State Office Building
Des Moines, Iowa 50319

KANSAS
State Department of Social Welfare
Child Welfare Services
State Office Building
Topeka, Kansas 66612

KENTUCKY
Department of Child Welfare
403 Wapping Street
Frankfort, Kentucky 40601

LOUISIANA
Child Welfare
Department of Public Welfare
P.O. Box 44065
Baton Rouge, Louisiana 70804

MAINE
Department of Health and Welfare
State House
Augusta, Maine 04330

181

MARYLAND
Social Services Administration–Department of Employment and Social Services
Family and Child Welfare Services
1100 North Eutow Street
Baltimore, Maryland 21201

MASSACHUSETTS
Massachusetts Department of Public Welfare
Social Services
Division of Family and Children's Services
600 Washington Street
Boston, Massachusetts 02111

MICHIGAN
State Department of Social Services
300 South Capitol
Lansing, Michigan 48926

MINNESOTA
Department of Public Welfare
Centennial Building
St. Paul, Minnesota 55755

MISSISSIPPI
State Department of Public Welfare
Division of Family and Children's Services
Box 4321
Fondren Station
Jackson, Mississippi 39216

MISSOURI
Division of Welfare
Family Services
615 E. 13th Street
Kansas City, Missouri 64104

MONTANA
Division of Social Services
State Department of Public Welfare
Helena, Montana 59601

NEBRASKA
Nebraska Department of Public Welfare
Division of Social Services
4900 "O"
Lincoln, Nebraska 68503

NEVADA
Department of Human Resources
Welfare Division
Family and Children's Services
251 Jeanell Drive
Capitol Mail Complex
Carson City, Nevada 89701

NEW HAMPSHIRE
State Department of Health and Welfare
Division of Welfare
Bureau of Child and Family Service
8 Loudon Road
Concord, New Hampshire 03301

NEW JERSEY
Department of Institutions and Agencies
Division of Youth and Family Services
Box 510
Trenton, New Jersey 08625

NEW MEXICO
Health and Social Services Department
Social Services Agency
Adoption Services
P.O. Box 2348
Santa Fe, New Mexico 87501

NEW YORK
New York State Department of Social Services
1450 Western Avenue
Albany, New York 12203

182

NORTH CAROLINA
Department of Human Resources
Department of Social Services
Children's Services Branch
325 N. Salisbury Street
Raleigh, North Carolina 27611

NORTH DAKOTA
Social Service Board of North Dakota
Capitol Building
Bismarck, North Dakota 58505

OHIO
Ohio Department of Public Welfare
Division of Social Services
Bureau of Services for Families and Children
30 East Broad Street
Columbus, Ohio 43215

OKLAHOMA
State Department of Institutions
Social and Rehabilitative Services
Division of Social Services
P.O. Box 25352
Oklahoma City, Oklahoma 73125

OREGON
Department of Human Resources
Children's Services Division
Adoption Department
509 Public Service Building
Salem, Oregon 97310

PENNSYLVANIA
State Department of Public Welfare
Bureau of Child Welfare
Health and Welfare Building
Harrisburg, Pennsylvania 17120

PUERTO RICO
Department of Social Services
Services to Families and Children
P.O. Box 11697
Fernandez Juncos Station
Santurce, Puerto Rico 00910

RHODE ISLAND
Rhode Island Child Welfare Service
610 Mount Pleasant Avenue
Providence, Rhode Island 02908

SOUTH CAROLINA
State Department of Public Welfare
Division of Children and Family Services
Box 1520
Columbia, South Carolina 29202

SOUTH DAKOTA
State Department of Public Welfare
Service Administrator
Pierre, South Dakota 57501

TENNESSEE
State Department of Public Welfare
Social Services
410 State Office Building
Nashville, Tennessee 37219

TEXAS
State Department of Public Welfare
John H. Regan Building
Austin, Texas 78701

UTAH
Utah Division of Family Services
333 So. Second East
Salt Lake City, Utah 84111

VERMONT
Vermont Department of Social and Rehabilitation Services
Children's Services Division
81 River St.
Montpelier, Vermont 05602

VIRGINIA
Department of Welfare
Division of Social Services
P.O. Box KM623288
Richmond, Virginia 23288

Directory of Adoption Resources

WASHINGTON
Department of Social and Health
Services
P.O. Box 1788
Olympia, Washington 98504

WISCONSIN
Department of Health and Social
Services
Division of Family Services
State Office Building
Madison, Wisconsin 53702

WEST VIRGINIA
West Virginia Department of Welfare
Division of Social Services
1900 Washington Street, East
Charleston, West Virginia 25305

WYOMING
Department of Health and Social
Services
Division of Public Assistance and
Social Services
State Office Building West
Cheyenne, Wyoming 82001

2. ADOPTION EXCHANGES

The adoption exchanges listed describe and picture children currently waiting for adoption and are periodically updated. To view one of the books write directly to the organization. Members will tell you how to obtain a copy or where to go to see a copy in your area, at a parents group or agency. Other adoption exchanges are being established around the country, such as those in Wisconsin, Delaware and Connecticut. Contact state and parent groups for information in your area.

AASK: Aid to the Adoption of Special Kids
P.O. Box 11212
Oakland, California 94611
(415) 547-1678

AASK is a nonprofit foundation founded by the DeBolt family of California, who have received national and international publicity because of their adoption of many children with major handicaps and their work in the field of child welfare. AASK is a rather special program of facilitation of adoptions for "special kids." A major part of its work is devoted to acting as intermediary between licensed adoption agencies and potential adoptive parents. Using all the resources listed here plus contacts with agencies that do not subscribe to listing services and more unorthodox contacts with people who write to AASK after hearing about the DeBolts, AASK attempts to bridge the information gap that often exists between parents and agencies.

AASK works only with families and agencies concerned with "special kids": children of minority background, children over nine years of age, children with medical problems, children who must have large numbers of siblings placed with them, and other children who may have to wait a long time for a permanent home.

184

Directory of Adoption Resources

AASK puts out a monthly newsletters available to the public, as well as offering direct aid to parents in locating children and securing financial and other assistance necessary in adoption.

ALSO: Adoption Listing Service of Ohio
  Council on Adoptable Children
  c/o Richard and Rose Lesh
  2216 40th Street
  Canton, Ohio 44709
  (216) 492-3604

ALSO lists children waiting for adoptive homes from all over the Ohio area; the book with pictures and descriptions is circulated to all agencies in the state and to parents and agencies in other areas. It is compiled and distributed on a periodic basis without charge.

ARENA: The Adoption Resource Exchange of North America
  67 Irving Place
  New York, New York 10003
  (212) 254-7410

ARENA is affiliated with the Child Welfare League of America, one of the major standard setters in adoption. Children who need adoptive homes and families who are searching for a child to adopt but have been unsuccessful at the local level are listed with ARENA by agencies from all over the United States and Canada in an effort to match these two links in adoption on a continentwide basis. Monthly newsletters sent to adoption agencies and parent groups contain pictures and descriptions of representative children, along with current information on the availability of adoptable children and adoptive homes. Most children registered with ARENA are considered by their local adoption agencies to be difficult to place in their own locale.

The CAP Book: A Manual of Waiting Children
  Council of Adoptive Parents
  425 Mt. Vernon Avenue
  Rochester, New York 14620
  (716) 473-7419

The CAP Book was started by a dedicated group of adoptive parents in upper New York State with the support and advice of adoption agencies. It is now funded by the New York State Department of Social Services.

Adoption agencies throughout New York can register adoptable children with the book. Each child is pictured on a separate page with a brief descriptive writeup. Agencies and adoptive applicants contact CAP for further information about any child listed in the current pages, which are updated every two to four weeks. Although the children are predominantly residents of New York, inquiries are encouraged from any state.

The CAP Book is not to be confused with the State Adoption Exchange in

185

New York, which lists children freed for adoption, without pictures, on a monthly basis, as mandated by state law. Cost of the CAP Book to subscribers is currently $15 per year.

Holt Adoption Book
Holt Adoption Program
P.O. Box 2420
Eugene, Oregon 97402
(503) 687-2202

The Holt Book, sometimes referred to as the "Blue Book" because of the color of its cover, contains pictures and descriptions of children in the custody of Holt Children's Services Adoption Program of Eugene, Oregon. The children from Korea, Vietnam, and elsewhere abroad are considered difficult to place because of age, racial background, medical problems, or number of siblings who must be placed together. Parents who inquire about these children usually must meet the standards for adoptive applicants set by the Holt Agency in order to have their inquiries seriously considered. Details can be found in Appendix H, International Adoption Information.

Illinois Multiple Listing Service
Child Care Association of Illinois
2101 West Laurence Avenue
Springfield, Illinois 62704
(217) 787-1715

The Child Care Association of Illinois, or CCA, is a listing service for families and children established by Rev. Charles Filson. The book works on the same principle as multiple listing in real estate, as do many of the exchanges: You can reach more people and benefit more children and families if you centralize and share all the available information and resources.

CCA lists waiting families with descriptions and preferences (without names or identifying data) and also lists waiting children with pictures and descriptions. These listings are predominantly from the Illinois area but inquiries are welcome from other states.

The MARE Book: Massachusetts Adoption Resource Exchange
600 Washington Street
Boston, Massachusetts 02111
(617) 727-6128

One of the functions of the Massachusetts Adoption Resource Exchange, known as MARE, is to compile and distribute a book listing waiting children, with pictures. As with most local exchanges, children pictured are largely in the custody of adoption agencies in that locale, but families and agencies outside the state may make inquiries.

186

The New York City Adoption Exchange Book
New York City Special Services for Children
80 Lafayette Street, 16th Floor
New York, New York 10013
(212) 433-7660

This exchange book is coordinated by the New York City public agency, Special Services for Children. Referred to as the "Red Book" because of its color, it lists only children available or potentially available for adoption from agencies within New York City. Inquiries about children described and pictured in the book are welcome from residents of any state. Most of the children listed are considered difficult to place by their agencies because they are of minority background (predominantly black), of school age, and/or have special needs because of physical, mental, or emotional handicaps.

C. Family Planning Resources

The following organizations can be of service to couples in the general area of family planning.

Planned Parenthood and World Population
National office: 810 Seventh Avenue
New York, New York 10019

This organization has centers in almost every urban area in the United States, as well as some suburban and rural communities. Services include contraception, abortion, vasectomy, and infertility service or referral.

The directory, *Planned Parenthood Affiliates*, can be obtained from the national office, or consult your local telephone directory under Planned Parenthood or Family Planning Resource Center.

RESOLVE
c/o Barbara Manning
14 Sargent Road
Belmont, Massachusetts 02178

RESOLVE is an informal support group for women that started on the East Coast. Its members deal with mutual problems and emotions concerning infertility, as well as related areas of miscarriage, stillbirth, and infant death. Lifestyle alternatives of childlessness and adoption may be explored. Information about RESOLVE groups or how to start one in your area can be obtained from the address above.

188

Zero Population Growth
1346 Connecticut Avenue S.W.
Washington, D.C. 20036

This nonprofit organization supports the view that the world's population should be controlled and limited through family planning. It advocates that couples who want a family limit their biological children to two, enough to replace only themselves and not add to an already overburdened planet.

NON: National Organization for Non-Parents
515 Madison Avenue
New York, New York 10022

NON is a nonprofit organization that offers support and encouragement to those who choose not to have children and those who choose to plan their families carefully. The group advocates "childfree" lifestyles as a realistic and socially acceptable option.

D. Counseling Services

If you want personal or family counseling prior to or after adoption, there are many resources you can tap. Parents groups and adoption agencies may be able to offer or refer you to some. Others may be available through your religious group, schools, or community hospital. A good starting point might be to contact the following organization, which has affiliates across the country:

Family Service Association of America
44 East 23rd Street
New York, New York 10010

Its *Directory of Member Agencies* is not available to the general public but members may be able to tell you of member agencies close to your home. Check your telephone directory for local listings under the following titles:

Health and Welfare Council	Council for Community Services
Community Chest	United Fund
Mental Health Clinic	Information and Referral Service
County Department of Health	Community Planning Council
Community Council	Counseling Clinic

Any of these may tell you of resources within your own community. But remember, not all professionals have experience or expertise in dealing with adoption. Try to determine this before you commit yourself to a particular program or individual. References from other clients can be quite helpful.

190

E. State Adoption Laws

The format of this general outline of state laws is based on a January 1973 U.S. Office of Child Development survey, which has been updated by a special questionnaire conducted by Information House. It should be noted that this is offered as a guide rather than a definitive directory, since policy shifts and statutory changes regarding adoption can occur in a state at any time.

The following did not respond to either the 1973 survey or the update by Information House, Inc.: Iowa, Rhode Island, South Dakota and Tennessee.

STATE OR COMMON-WEALTH	PERMITS INDEPENDENT PLACEMENT	PERMITS INDEPENDENT ADOPTION	OFFERS SUBSIDY	REQUIRES JUDICIAL TERMINATION OF PARENTAL RIGHTS
Alabama	Yes	Yes	Decided in each case	No
Alaska	Yes	Yes	No	Yes
Arizona	Yes	Yes	medical	No
Arkansas	Disapproves but not prohibited		medical	No
California	By bio parents only		in some cases	In some cases
Colorado	parental consent revokable for one year after placement		medical; boarding	
Connecticut	Only by approved agencies outside state		Yes	Yes

191

STATE OR COMMON-WEALTH	PERMITS INDEPENDENT PLACEMENT	PERMITS INDEPENDENT ADOPTION	OFFERS SUBSIDY	REQUIRES JUDICIAL TERMINATION OF PARENTAL RIGHTS
Delaware	No	No	Boarding, legal	Yes
D.C.	No By bio parent, relative or guardian only	Yes	Yes	In some cases
Florida	Yes	Yes	No	Yes
Georgia	Yes investigation required	No	boarding, special	No
Hawaii	Yes	Yes	In some cases	Yes
Idaho	Yes	Yes	medical	Yes
Illinois	Yes	No	medical, boarding, legal, special	Yes
Indiana	No	No	medical, boarding	No
Iowa	presently under re-examination	medical; boarding	Yes	No
Kansas	Yes	Yes	medical, boarding	Yes
Kentucky	With approval of Comm. of Child Welfare		boarding, in special cases	No
Louisiana	Yes	Yes	No	No
Maine	No, except by bio parents	Yes with study by lic. agency	legislation pending	Not always
Maryland	By bio parent or relative		medical; boarding	Yes
Massachusetts	Yes, must report to state dept.	Yes	medical; boarding	
Michigan	Within state only by court or licensed agency	No	medical; boarding	Yes

192

Directory of Adoption Resources

STATE OR COMMON-WEALTH	PERMITS INDEPENDENT PLACEMENT	PERMITS INDEPENDENT ADOPTION	OFFERS SUBSIDY	REQUIRES JUDICIAL TERMINATION OF PARENTAL RIGHTS
Minnesota	No	No, unless court allows	medical; boarding	Yes
Mississippi	Yes	Yes	not specified	No, accepts voluntary consent
Missouri	Some courts permit		medical; boarding	In some cases
Montana	Yes	Yes	For handi-capped children	Yes
Nebraska	By bio parent or court		medical; boarding	No
Nevada	No	No	medical; boarding	No
New Hampshire	Yes	No	No, rare exceptions	Yes
New Jersey	With bio parent consent	No	med., boarding legal, special	Yes, for non-relatives
New Mexico	Yes, but leg. pending for prohibition	No, but law can be waived	legislation pending	No
New York	Yes	Yes	med., boarding, other special	No
North Carolina	Yes, but not encouraged	No	No, rare exceptions	No
North Dakota	No	Yes	medical; boarding	No
Ohio	Yes, with consent of court or dept. of welfare		med., boarding, legal, special	Yes
Oklahoma	Yes	Yes	only prior to finalization	No
Oregon	By bio relative only		boarding	No, legis. pending
Pennsylvania	Yes	Yes	medical; boarding	Yes
Puerto Rico	No	No; study by Dept. Social Svs.	No	Yes

Directory of Adoption Resources

STATE OR COMMON-WEALTH	PERMITS INDEPENDENT PLACEMENT	PERMITS INDEPENDENT ADOPTION	OFFERS SUBSIDY	REQUIRES JUDICIAL TERMINATION OF PARENTAL RIGHTS
Rhode Island			Yes	
South Carolina	Yes	Yes	not specified	Agency requires, Law does not
South Dakota			Yes	Yes
Tennessee			Yes	Yes
Texas	Yes	Yes	Boarding	Yes
Utah	Yes	Yes	medical	Yes
Vermont	Yes, but legislation pending to prohibit		med., boarding, other special	Yes
Virginia	Bio relative, guardian, step-parent only except with approval of Comm.		limited med., boarding	In some cases
Washington	Yes	No	legislation pending	Yes
West Virginia	Yes	Yes	No	No
Wisconsin	Only with court approval	No, agency assigned by court	medical	Yes
Wyoming	Yes, but legislation pending to alter this		not at present	Yes

SOURCE: Information House questionnaire survey, November 1974. © Copyright Information House, Inc., 1975.

NOTE: Most adoption subsidies are limited to children considered by the state in which they reside to be "hard-to-place." This definition differs from state to state.

Eligibility for most, but not all, state adoption subsidies is determined in part by the income of the prospective adoptive parents. Each district, county or city may have the power to recommend to the state that the subsidy be granted to a particular family for the adoption of a "hard-to-place" child.

Most states do not have residency requirements for parents requesting adoption subsidies. This means, for example, that a couple in Ohio could adopt a child previously living in New York and be eligible for a N.Y. state adoption subsidy.

F. Recent Legislation and Court Decisions on Adoption

1. ADOPTION IN THE COURTS

The following court decisions have set precedents affecting other adoptions.

Parental Rights

• The famous "Baby Lenore" case in 1971 was one of the most publicized custody cases in adoption. An infant girl, born to an unwed mother who signed surrender papers with the Spence-Chapin adoption agency, was placed for adoption by the agency with the DeMartino family. The child's biological mother, Olga Scarpetta, reversed her decision to surrender the child shortly after the child was placed and took the adoption agency to court after it refused to return the child. But it was not until almost eighteen months later, with a court decision directing them to return the child, that the prospective adoptive parents were told of any of this. The decision was upheld by the higher courts and the DeMartinos fled to Florida, where the courts decided in their favor.

The controversy stirred up by this case ultimately led to a New York State law stating that after thirty days a biological mother's release for adoption of her child is irrevocable. Other states also have taken a closer look at their surrender provisions as a result of this case.

• With new precedents being set by foster care legislation and court cases, increasing numbers of foster parents are contesting custody when their foster children have been in their homes for long periods of time. And when children are released for adoption, more foster parents are receiving priority as prospective adoptive parents.

195

One significant court ruling came in a 1973 custody case, one of the first cases where the courts denied custody to both the child welfare agency and the bio parent and awarded it to the foster parents.

Mr. and Mrs. James Tingstrum had had a foster daughter in their home for over nine years, since shortly after her birth, and were contesting her return to her biological mother. In the opinion of the presiding judge, Tim Murphy, the child's best interests were the essential consideration, not the rights or desires of any adults—be they biological, foster, or adoptive parents. In this particular case it was felt that the child's best interests were met by the continuation of established family ties with the Tingstrums.

• Since the early 1970s numerous challenges have arisen over the parental rights of the "unwed father." One case in Illinois, Stanley versus Illinois, involved a man denied custody of his biological children when his common-law wife died, even though he had materially and psychologically acted as their parent. A Supreme Court ruling of April 4, 1972, decided that alleged bio fathers must have the right to a court hearing on custody of contested children and that all children have two legal parents, regardless of the marital status of those parents.

In a second case, Lewis-Rothstein, an unwed mother terminated her parental rights to her child without telling the child's bio father, who was denied a hearing on his termination of parental rights. This case also was referred to the Supreme Court but remanded back to the Wisconsin Supreme Court with orders to reconsider its first decision that the unwed father had no rights to a hearing in view of the Stanley case recommendations. It also was suggested that in cases arising after April 4, 1972, the length of time a child had been in the adoptive home should be a consideration in the final decision.

Other cases arose after this one, in situations where the bio mother terminated her rights after April 4, 1972, and the alleged bio fathers were not advised at the time that they had any rights. If the courts find that these rights were violated and bio fathers have the right to a hearing, under current practices they must be declared legally the child's bio father and be shown fit to raise the child. During this time, the bio mother often can make a reconsideration of her prior termination and make a claim for parental rights. But if the current trend holds, the well-being of the child will be the primary consideration.

Adoptions made before April 4, 1972, would not be affected and most adoption judges are being meticulous about correct procedures in current cases to avoid future challenges. There has been a legal defense fund established to help parents involved in custody challenges by the Open Door Society of Milwaukee, Wisconsin.

• A 1973 California case held that prospective adoptive parents involved with the placement of a child for adoption have the right to a hearing on a change in their status by a placement agency. Parents also are entitled to notice prior to proposed termination of placement, except in extraordinary cases where there is danger to the child's health and safety.

196

The overriding considerations in such a case, ruled the California Court of Appeals, should be facts relative to the child's best interests, not the agency's abuse of discretionary powers.

Religion

• Placement of children for adoption across religious lines has been a bone of contention for several decades. Recently, most states and courts seem to interpret liberally religious requirements of adoption statutes, if they exist, in light of the child's total welfare.

In a 1958 case the New York Court of Appeals interpreted the religious provisions of the law as discretionary. The child's bio mother was contesting the proposed adoption on the grounds that she was Catholic and the prospective parents were Protestant. Since the child had been fostered in their home for almost four years, the court awarded custody to the prospective adoptive parents, seeing this as in the best interests of the child's total well-being. While there have been decisions upholding religious matching, recent cases have increasingly followed the lead of the 1958 decision.

• In late 1970 an adoption was refused by the courts in New Jersey solely because the prospective adoptive parents did not have a belief in an established religion. Both the placement agency and the biological parents of the child had consented to the adoption. The decision was reversed in 1971 by a higher court that declared that it may be unconstitutional to deny adoption solely because of a lack of belief in an established religion or a supreme being.

Race

• A Texas prohibition on interracial adoption was struck down in 1967 by the Court of Civil Appeals in the case of a black man who had been disqualified to adopt his white wife's children. The opinion of the court was based on sixteen years of civil rights cases with rulings that racial discrimination is a violation of the equal protection and due process clauses of the Fourteenth Amendment. Statutes prohibiting adoption across racial lines are considered unconstitutional.

• A suit was filed in Ohio by Susan and Richard Chartoff against a public welfare agency that, it was claimed, discriminated against both adoptive parents and children by its policy that only blacks were eligible to apply for the children available at the agency, who were black.

The agency, Montgomery County Children's Services, decided not to risk a court test and agreed to accept and process adoption applications regardless of race. The family involved agreed both to drop the suit to have previous agency policy declared unconstitutional and to have an injunction issued against the practice.

197

2. PENDING FEDERAL LEGISLATION RELATING TO ADOPTION

Sponsor	*Purpose*
Rep. Esch	To establish a computerized National Adoption Information Exchange.
Sen. Randolph	Same as above.
Rep. Rarick	To amend Internal Revenue Code of 1954 to allow deduction of adoption expenses.
Rep. Corman	To allow deduction of adoption expenses up to $1,250.
Rep. Frenzel	To allow deduction of up to $1,500 in adoption expenses for first adopted child and $1,000 for additional children.
Rep. Talcott	To allow deduction of all "reasonable and necessary" adoption expenses.
Rep. Hanley	Same as above.
Rep. Brown, Mich.	To allow deductions of adoption expenses up to $750.
Sen. Young	To allow deduction of all adoption expenses.
Sen. Inouye	To allow deduction of adoption expenses up to $1,000.
Rep. Koch	To grant an alien child adopted by a single parent the same immigrant status as one adopted by a couple.
Rep. Sisk	Same as above; also provides for granting immediate relative status to more than two adopted children.
Rep. Edwards, Calif.	To amend the Immigration and Naturalization Act to reduce to one year the waiting period for naturalization of a child adopted by a U.S. citizen.
Rep. Mink	To provide special immigrant status to American-fathered orphans.
Rep. Steiger	To confer U.S. citizenship on American-fathered children and to simplify adoption procedures.
Rep. Kastenmeier	To provide assistance to improve the welfare of Vietnamese children and facilitate their adoption.
Rep. Dulski	Same as above.

3. EXAMPLES OF RECENT STATE LEGISLATION

As an example of recent legislation on the state level, here are some bills passed into law in 1974 by the New York State Legislature. Some states may

198

be more advanced and already have similar laws on the books, others may lag behind, but this is the trend.

S. 8408–A/A. 9918–A: Amends Social Services Law, authorizing public welfare commissioners and city public welfare officers to enter into contract with adoptive parents of children with handicaps for payments of medical, etc., expenses until the child is twenty-one or to make payments of such expenses without contract without regard to financial ability of adoptive parents.

S. 8595–A/A. 10371–A: Amends Social Services Law to require social services departments to prepare for the legislature annually a written evaluation report of their delivery of child welfare services.

S. 8615/A. 10374: Provides for adoption subsidy payments to continue if child is moved to another state or adopted by residents of another state or Puerto Rico.

The following bills were vetoed by the governor of New York in 1974 but may be introduced in future years:

S8428B/A9924B: Would mandate setting of standards for acceptance or rejection of adoptive applicants by agencies and an appeals mechanism for violation of standards.

S8614A/A10375A: Would provide up to $1,000 on a one-time basis to be paid to preserve a bio family rather than offering foster care as the only alternative to a family in crisis.

S9974/Rules Committee: Would require state department of Social Services to give written notice to concerned parties of a change in regulations thirty days prior to such a change.

G. International Adoption Information

1. GENERAL PROCEDURE

Each international adoption is somewhat different, even adoptions arranged by the same agency, but there are some usual steps that almost everyone attempting to adopt from abroad will take. They are outlined here in broad form. You will of course have to get specific information from whatever contact you use about particular programs.

First, however we should mention the general types of international contacts for adoption:

1. Adoption through an established licensed agency in the United States.

2. Adoption through an agency abroad, perhaps with the aid of a formal or informal U.S. contact or support group.

3. An independent adoption arranged directly by the adoptive parents and/or their lawyer with a foreign contact such as an orphanage director, doctor, lawyer, personal friend, or others. These do not usually ask for a homestudy.

In all three types, the aim is to locate, legally obtain custody of, adopt, and bring into the United States on a permanent basis a child, usually orphaned or abandoned, who is not a U.S. citizen.

Steps to take:

1. Check with your state department of welfare or other state agency governing adoptions: What are the adoption regulations of your state? What are the policies governing foreign adoptions? Are there specific agencies to contact or policies to follow? If you do not meet these requirements, you may

200

not be able to obtain a preferential visa for your child (which saves a long wait on a quota list) unless you physically see the child before applying for a visa. For a couple, this means that both of you will have to travel to see the child.

2. Starting with local agencies first, find out which licensed adoption agencies in your state will do homestudies for foreign adoptions. In some areas, public agencies will do these; in other areas, only private agencies will. Agencies also vary as to what types of foreign placements they will handle and which international agencies they will work with. If you plan to move across state lines, check with your new state about regulations and whether your homestudy will be transferrable.

3. At the same time, contact groups working with foreign adoptions. Some private (independent) contacts may not ask for homestudies, but your state still may. Agencies abroad may ask after they assign a child to you rather than before. Sometimes local adoption agencies will not do a homestudy for you until you are accepted as a prospective adoptive parent by an international program. But some international programs will not accept you until you can show a completed study. This type of situation can be circumvented by having one write a letter to the other saying that you would be considered for adoption pending their action.

4. Narrow down to three or four programs that interest you and write to them for information. Based on their replies, choose two that fit your needs, and that you also fit as an applicant, and apply. But notify them that you wish to apply to other programs. If neither works out, try your next choices.

5. After one of the programs accepts your application, asks for and receives your homestudy; or after your homestudy is sent to the program with your application and you are approved; or after you have sent preliminary papers to a foreign contact or agency and been approved—you will *wait*. How long you wait depends upon the program, the available children, and your requests and background.

6. Finally, information on a child, and usually a picture, is sent to you either directly or through your agency or lawyer. If for good reason you decide that you cannot accept this child, you will possibly be assigned another child at a later date. If you accept a child, documents will be exchanged so that you can begin the adoption and immigration proceedings. With many foreign contacts, you will be required to travel to pick up the child and may have to spend time in the child's country to arrange legal matters. U.S. agencies do not usually require this.

7. Contact the nearest U.S. Immigration and Naturalization Office to determine the type of visa your child will need for entry in to the United States. Most couples will obtain an I-600 form, "Petition to Classify Orphan as Immediate Relative." It asks for a preferential visa on the basis that an orphaned or half-orphaned child under the age of fourteen will be adopted by a couple at least one of whom is a citizen. A couple will fill it out and submit it with: child's birth certificate, parents' birth certificates, proof of orphanage, fingerprints of parents, marriage certificate, and financial statements. An I-600 takes four to eight weeks to process normally, and a health

201

check must be done by a U.S. Public Health Service official on the child abroad. Families who will travel abroad and see the child do not have to prove they meet state requirements for adoption and may shorten processing time.

8. You will not be able to use an I-600 visa if: you are single; you have already used two I-600 visas; neither spouse is a citizen; the child has two living parents; the child is over fourteen. Unless you are willing to wait out the quota, you must find some other type of preferential visa such as medical students, visitors, or special act of Congress introduced by your congressman.

9. When the papers have been approved by immigration officials, they are sent or you bring them to the U.S. consul nearest your child overseas. The consul then has the power to issue the visa.

10. Once the visa has been issued and an exit visa issued to the child by the foreign country of which he is a citizen, *and* if all the adoption proceedings or other necessary matters as outlined by the program or contact are completed, your child is ready to go home.

11. How long it takes to prepare for the journey depends upon the health of the child, how efficient the program is, and the avaiablility of escorts and flights. If you escort your own child, you should make sure you both have passports and identification in order.

12. After arrival in the United States, you must register your child as an alien every January with the INS since he or she is not a citizen.

13. After a minimum of six months you can file for legal adoption of your child in your state of residence. The adoption proceedings may differ slightly from domestic adoptions, so check with your courts.

14. Two years after legal adoption, your child is eligible for naturalization as a U.S. citizen.

2. INTERNATIONAL ADOPTION CONTACTS

The following groups process families who want to adopt a child from abroad, and some can provide additional information regarding other sources of adoptable children. Most will require that a prospective parent contact a local adoption agency for a homestudy. Contact each for current policies.

David Livingston Missionary Foundation Adoption Program
P.O. Box 232
Tulsa, Oklahoma 74101
(918) 836-1692

The David Livingston Missionary Foundation sponsors an adoption program for Korean orphans which is administered by Dillon Family and Youth Services of Tulsa, Oklahoma, a child-placing agency licensed by the state of Oklahoma and jointly licensed with the Foundation by the Korean government for intercountry adoptions in the United States. Children available are from six months to thirteen years of age.

202

Directory of Adoption Resources

Applicant policies:

1. An applicant couple must be married at least two years.
2. Only married couples are eligible.
3. Only U.S. citizens are eligible.
4. Both prospective parents must be living in the United States at the time of the application.
5. The Foundation states: "We have no restriction regarding religious preference of adoptive applicants although it is important to us that a child be taught religious principles. We believe that adoptive parents who have religious convictions and practice these principles usually have more stability in their home life."
6. Applicants should be in good health.
7. Only one child is placed with a family at a time except in the case of siblings.
8. Children fourteen and older cannot be adopted.
9. If you have been divorced, you should be remarried at least four years before applying for adoption.
10. According to new Korean regulations regarding adoptions, there can be no more than forty years and no less than twenty years difference in age between adoptive parents and child. Exceptions can sometimes be made in the case of children considered difficult to place.
11. A family with five or more children presently living in their home is ineligible to adopt under new Korean regulations. Children not living in the home are not counted in the total number of children. Exceptions can be made only with hard-to-place children on occasion.

Cost: Total legal, processing, and travel costs for adoption from Livingston are included in a flat fee of $950, of which $100 is sent with the application. If for some reason your application is denied, $75 will be returned. There is no refund for withdrawals. A check for $400 accompanies documents after you have agreed upon a child offered to you, and the final $400 is due when U.S. Immigration approval for the visa is received.

Adoption procedure: After your application is approved, you will be required to obtain a homestudy from a local licensed agency. After the study is completed and submitted to Dillon Family and Youth Services, which handles the adoption procedures for the Livingston Program, you will be notified through the homestudy agency whether or not you are approved for placement and a child will be selected for you. Dillion Family and Youth Services will do homestudies for families in the Tulsa area for an additional fee.

Applications are considered within a month after the application is received by the program, but there is now a short waiting list for applicants requesting a child under two. The entire adoption process from homestudy to arrival of a child will take around nine to eleven months.

Approximate number of annual placements: 250.

Families for Children
10 Bowling Green
Pointe Claire, 720
Quebec, Canada
(514) 697-7296

FFC is a licensed Canadian adoption agency organized by adoptive parents that helps prospective adoptive parents in arranging adoptions. It will assist parents by locating a child for adoption and guiding parents through the proper procedure for legal adoption and immigration of the child to the United States, or to Canada. FFC also works cooperatively with its affiliate, the Friends For All Children agency in Colorado.

Applicant Policies:

An up-to-date homestudy by a recognized agency in your area is required prior to formal application, and in some cases, where distance permits, a family will be asked to travel to Quebec for an interview.

FFC asks that parents requesting assistance have no stipulations regarding race. Many of the children known to the agency are of minority or mixed-racial background, including Black, American Indian, Oriental, and Indian. There is a particular need for parents who can accept children with handicaps. FFC will not work with parents whose religon restricts medical treatment.

Cost:

Fees and procedures depend on the country and the contacts used; the usual approximate cost for all legal and travel expenses is $1000. FFC itself is staffed entirely by volunteers so there are no direct agency fees to FFC. In some countries child support is required during the period when the child is waiting to leave his or her country of origin for a new home.

Placement:

FFC makes placements of children from the following countries: India, Bangladesh, Vietnam, and other parts of Southeast Asia, the Philippines, Ecuador, and occasionally from other countries.

Approximate number of annual placements: 250.

Foreign Adoption Center, Inc.
P.O. Box 2158
Boulder, Colorado 80302

The Foreign Adoption Center is a licensed child placement agency that provides information and assistance to adoptive parents and agencies as well as concrete adoption help in the form of child placement. It is unique among the licensed agencies in this dual role of information and placement. FAC is a central information resource for foreign adoptions, particularly for the ever-changing independent adoption contacts like Paraiso Infantil, FANA, the Haiti Project, Baja Children's Foundation, Casa de la Madre y el Nino, and others. As part of its information services, it offers a pamphlet costing $3 that outlines the general overseas adoption picture, and also more detailed pamphlets on specific countries. FAC is entirely staffed by volunteers from the United States and in foreign countries who operate as staff members and advisors.

Applicant Policies:

1. Each applicant must be above the age of twenty-one years.
2. Couples must have been married for one year or more.
3. The age difference between the requested child and each adopting parent must be less than forty years.
4. The adopting mother must not have full-time employment for one year following placement of a child. Part-time employment plans will be considered on an individual basis.
5. One year or more must lapse between the placement of a child/children and another application to adopt again.

Cost:

For children placed by FAC there is a processing fee. Total costs, including FAC fees, air fare, and lawyers fees range from $800 to $1350, depending upon the country and contact used. An initial application fee of $15 is submitted with the application.

Placement:

Placements are being made from Colombia and Guatemala, and future placements will include children from infants to adolescence from Haiti, Honduras, India, Korea, Nicaragua, Peru, and Thailand. There is a need for homes for children six and older.

Approximate number of annual placements: under 100, but will be increasing gradually.

Friends for All Children
445 South 68th Street
Boulder, Colorado 80302
(303) 495-7305

FFAC is a licensed adoption agency staffed by volunteers in Colorado and Vietnam, placing children for adoption primarly from the orphanages of Rosemary Taylor in Saigon and the provinces, and also from Cambodia.

Applicant Policies:

Each applicant is considered individually rather than by set standards of eligibility. Single applicants are generally not considered except for those children difficult to place otherwise. A homestudy from an agency licensed by the applicants state of residence is required after the formal application

205

is submitted, as is the cover (1040) sheet of the previous year's tax form, to determine fees.

Cost:

FFAC has a $100 non-refundable application fee, $75 to be applied to the adoption fee. The adoption fee is based on income, ranging from $100 for families with a taxable income below $9000 to $500 for families over $24,000. Fees are paid within two weeks of acceptance of a child.

Airfare is not included in the adoption fee, and neither is a $150 legal fee for adoption work in Vietnam, also payable within two weeks of acceptance of a child for adoption.

Adoption Procedure:

1. Applicants are sent a form to fill out and return to FFAC after they inquire about adoption, which asks about applicants' interest in particular types of children.
2. Applicants are put on waiting lists according to the date and the type of child desired.
3. An application is sent when a family's name reaches the top of their list, from a few weeks up to a year of waiting.
4. When the application is returned, evaluated, and formally accepted by FFAC a homestudy is requested.
5. If a family decides to contact some other agency to locate a child at any point FFAC must be notified.
6. The wait for a child to arrive after applications have been received is six months to fifteen months, which includes the time taken to locate the type of child desired, process for adoption and immigration, and arrange for transportation.

Placement:

The wait for placement is considerably longer for couples requesting only girls, particularly for infants. FFAC is seeking more homes for siblings, post-polio, cleft-palate, blind, deaf, emotionally disturbed and slow-learning children of Vietnamese and Vietnamese-American background.

Approximate number of annual placements: 350.

Friends of Children of Vietnam
600 Gilpin Street
Denver, Colorado 80218
(303) 321-8251

FCVN is a licensed adoption agency staffed by volunteers working with children from orphanages in Vietnam. It has parent chapters around the United States that assist with fund-raising to help support the children in care, and with prospective adoptive parent education and aid.

Applicant Policies:

Applicants are considered individually in light of the needs of the children to be placed, and the judgement of the homestudy agency. Single parents and handicapped parents are acceptable as applicants, and FCVN will consider placing more than one child at a time with a family.

Cost:

A $25 non-refundable fee is required to accompany the application form sent by FCVN after an initial wait determined by the type of child indicated on the preliminary forms. The "Child Care/Processing Fee" is based on income reported on the 1040 tax form and is payable within thirty days of the acceptance of a particular child offered. Fees range from $200 for incomes under $10,000 to $600 for incomes over $25,000. Plane fare is not included in the processing fee, and it averages around $400, payable within thirty days after acceptance of a child.

Adoption Procedure:

Parents are sent a preliminary form to determine their interests, and how fast they can be processed for a child. They are sent a formal application to fill out when children of the type they desire become available, and a homestudy is sent to FCVN after the application is formally accepted. The wait for placement after the acceptance is between six and eighteen months.

Placement:

Children available for adoption range in age from infants to around eight years of age and are Vitenamese, Vietnamese-Black, or Vietnamese-Caucasian. Homes are particularly needed for boys, for handicapped children, and for children of school age.

Approximate number of annual placements: 150-200.

Friends of Children, Inc.
14 Brookside Road
Darien, Connecticut 06820
(203) 655-2218

Friends of Children is licensed in the state of Connecticut and their adoption service is called the Rosemary Taylor Agency, after the dedicated woman who has been working for so many years with Vietnamese children. They do homestudies, not direct placements. They are presently the only Connecticut agency helping to place Vietnamese children.

Applicant Policies:

Applicants who wish to have a homestudy done by this agency should reside in the state of Connecticut and be willing to work with either the Holt or FFAC agencies for placement of a Vietnamese child. Single or married applicants should be no less than 18 years older than the child they wish to apply for, and no more than 44 years older, and married couples should be married at least two years prior to application. Prospective parents should be willing to accept children in varying degrees of physical health, due to the poor orphanage conditions.

Costs:

The homestudy fee to Rosemary Taylor Agency is $650: $100 application fee, $300 due at the completion of the study, and five monthly payments of $50 each. To this is added the transportation cost of the child and the International Agency Fee. (See FFAC and Holt for specifics.)

Adoption Procedure:

Applicants are advised to first write to FFAC and Holt for information and applications, and then to telephone the Rosemary Taylor Agency with a formal request for a homestudy after the material has been reviewed. There is about a six month wait before a homestudy can be started, and usually a six month wait after that before a child is assigned. Once a child is assigned the wait until arrival is anywhere from three to six months. The homestudy itself generally takes two to three months.

Placement:

Homes are particularly needed for children over the age of six, and for handicapped children, especially for boys. There are many abandoned infants available, but most applicants request infants. No consideration will be given to an application for a specifically Caucasian/Vietnamese child. Placements are made in conjunction with Friends for All Children and Holt Children's Services.

Approximate number of annual placements: presently 25, but will be increasing.

Holt Adoption Program
P.O. Box 2420
Eugene, Oregon 94702
(503) 687-2202

The Holt Adoption Program started in the early 1950s and has since grown to the largest adoption agency in the world, in 1974 placing almost 3,000 children from five countries with families in every state, with Americans abroad, and in eight foreign countries.

Applicant Policies:

Holt must follow the new laws governing Korean adoptions, as mentioned in the description of the Livingston Program. These deal with age and family size. Other guidelines include:

1. Applicants must be at least twenty-one years of age.
2. Parents must have some prior experience in dealing with children of the age they request, such as teaching, family, or other exposure.

208

3. Normally, infants are not placed with applicants over forty.

4. Couples should be married for at least two years.

5. It is recommended that there be a year difference in the age of your children and the planned adopted child.

6. In the event of an unanticipated pregnancy, Holt will postpone without prejudice the adoptive request.

7. Holt will not consider a second application until at least the first child is adopted, usually six months after arrival.

8. Working parents should schedule at least a six months' leave of absence for one of them, for the sake of the child's proper adjustment.

9. At least one of the parents should be a U.S. citizen.

10. Only couples are eligible.

11. Families must write a statement of faith, their relationship with God.

Costs:

The adoption processing fee, which does not include transportation costs, currently is 4 percent of a family's adjusted gross income, with a maximum fee of $1,000. For two siblings the fee is 150 percent of the fee schedule for that family's income; for three it is 180 percent. If Holt does the actual homestudy and postplacement visits in New Jersey and Oregon, there will be an extra charge. Fees can be waived or reduced for certain children considered difficult to place, usually handicapped children or mixed-race children of school age.

Adoption Procedure:

There is currently a waiting list for young children; about a year for infants. Prior to receiving an application that should be accompanied by a $10 nonrefundable fee when returned, you will get a preliminary information blank. It is reviewed by Holt for immediate or deferred processing, depending on whether or not you could accept a hard-to-place child.

If you can accept a hard-to-place child, your application will be sent more quickly. Holt will consider waiving or reducing fees for a child with a major handicap or a school-aged mixed race child.

After the application has been accepted, a homestudy is requested by Holt from an agency licensed in the applicants' state of residence. A child is usually offered to a couple within two months after the homestudy is received and approved by Holt. After the child has been formally accepted by the family as the prospective adoptive child, it takes three to six months before the child arrives in the home.

Placement:

Most placements are of children from Korea, and recently from Vietnam, but small numbers of children have come from South America and the Philippines. Holt adoptions have increased almost 50 percent each year. In 1962 a total of 152 children were placed; a decade later in 1972 the total was 2 014 children.

209

The 1974 report states that "boys are waiting from six months to more than a year and half longer than girls for a home." Also in need of homes are children of school age, and children with handicaps or medical problems.

Approximate annual number of placements: 2000, with another 1700 outside of the U.S.

Lutheran Social Service of Minnesota
2414 Park Avenue
Minneapolis, Minnesota 55404
(612) 339-0821

LSS is a licensed adoption agency that places Korean children for adoption with families in cooperation with Korea Social Service, a licensed Korean placement agency.

Applicant Policies:

LSS works only with residents of the state of Minnesota who are both members of an Evangelical Christian Church. Single parents are not considered. Priority for children under six goes to childless and one-child families "where the age differential between the oldest member of the couple and the child they seek to adopt is not more than thirty-five years."

Cost:

There is a $600 fee to LSS, plus a fee to the referral agency and transportation for the child, so that inter-country adoptions usually total $1,200 to $1,500. These fees can be reduced in some cases.

Adoption Procedure:

LSS does the homestudy for the family and placement is done in cooperation with KSS, to place children of Korean and occasionally of Korean-American background.

Approximate number of annual placements: under 100.

My Friends' House
161 Auburn Street
Newton, Massachusetts 02166
(617) 965-2320

MFH arranges adoptions of Vietnamese children, with priority given to Amerasian children, older children, and handicapped children. They will also do homestudies for certain other children placed by other agencies, considered difficult to place for applicants 23 or over living within 1½ hours drive from Boston or Newton, Massachusetts.

210

Directory of Adoption Resources

Applicant Policies:

MFH tries to evaluate applicants on their own merits and strengths rather than set up specific restrictions on family size, race, religion and so forth. It is preferred that couples be married at least two years and be no more than forty years older than the child they seek to adopt. MFH will do home-studies for prospective single parents only if they are willing to locate and process all legal work for a child themselves.

Homestudies for families outside of an hour and a half commute from Boston or Newton, Massachusetts must come from an agency other than MFH, which must also accept responsibility for follow-up and placement fail-ure (only Vietnamese children ages one to four with a medical problem for these). Because of the agency's commitment to serve children with the great-est need, applications cannot be accepted from couples who wish to avoid certain racial backgrounds.

Cost:

Fees, exclusive of transportation, are based on income and number of children in family. Homestudy fees range from $300 to $400, plus processing fees of $450 to $1500 when MRH processes a child itself. If MHF does the study for a child placed by another agency, add that agency's fee to the MFH homestudy fee. There is a flat fee of $350 for post-placement counsel-ing and legal adoption in the U.S. If another agency provides this service, MFH fees would not apply except for processing and child care. A $50 non-refundable fee is to accompany the application. One-half the total amount is due when a child is assigned; and the final half, less the application fee, when the child arrives. If you reside in eastern Massachusetts and MFH does the homestudy or update of an old homestudy for you, there will be an additional fee.

Placement:

MFH will place with applicants outside of their commuting distance only Vietnamese children under school age, the children they have in custody in their reception center in Vietnam. These children usually have significant medical, physical, or emotional-mental difficulties, and are a various racial mixes (Vietnamese-Black, Vietnamese-Caucasian, or full Vietnamese).

For applicants over 23 who are within the hour and half commuting dis-tance, MFH will do the homestudy and be responsible for the post placement counselling and legal work of children for whom a "waiting list does not exist": the older, handicapped, mixed race, black, or otherwise hard to place child.

Approximate number of annual placements: 30-50.

Pearl Buck Foundation
29 Delancy Place
Philadelphia, Pennsylvania 19103
(303) 443-3569

This foundation, not to be confused with Welcome House, which also was founded by Pearl Buck, is developing an adoption program for Amerasian children. It is working in Vietnam, Thailand, and possibly will be placing from Taiwan or other countries. Most children available will be under five years of age.

Travelers Aid—International Social Service of America
345 East 46th Street
New York, New York 10017
(212) 687-2747

TAISSA, formerly known as ISS, has a very limited adoption program in the Far East. It places children from Korea and Vietnam; for couples of Chinese and Japanese heritage only it will place some children from Hong Kong and Japan. Fees are in the vicinity of $350 to $550 depending on the income of applicants and the costs of the care and processing abroad. Transportation and escort costs are not included in that figure. TAISSA does not do homestudies.

United States Catholic Conference
Migration and Refugee Services
201 Park Avenue South
New York, New York 10003
(212) 475-5400

The USCC operates a very small intercountry adoption program for Vietnamese children. It functions solely through the over 150 local Catholic Charities' offices in the United States. Parents are responsible for all processing and legal costs; there is no set fee except as is determined by each local Catholic Charities adoption arm.

Welcome House
P.O. Box 836
Doylestown, Pennsylvania 18901
(215) 345-0430

Welcome House was originally established to place oriental and part-oriental American children in adoptive homes, but now places only foreign born children, primarily from Korea. It is licensed as an adoption agency in the following states: New York, New Jersey, Pennsylvania, Connecticut, Maryland, Delaware, Virginia, and the District of Columbia. Placements are usually made within a two-hundred-mile radius to facilitate the homestudy and supervision by Welcome House staff.

Applicant Policies:

Parents who do not live within this 200 mile radius distance must be able to obtain a homestudy from a local agency to be sent to Welcome House, and the agency must be willing to supervise the placement and final adoption proceedings. In that case, the parents do not have to pay the adoption service fee but merely an adoption referral fee of $300 plus transportation and legal costs. The only children available to out-of-area residents are Korean children.

Parents within the radius of 200 miles can consider the adoption of Canadian Indian children; this involves parents personally going to Toronto to pick up the child.

Welcome House will accept an application that limits preference to girls only if the family applying has sons but no daughters. Childless couples cannot limit themselves to a girl and should consider children up to and including two years of age: couples who request a child under a year will probably be disappointed. Parents should be no less than 21 years older than the child they seek to adopt and no more than 40 years older. Parents are required to have cash savings of $2,500 to $3,000 at the time of application.

Cost:

Fee payments for families range from $150 for families with incomes below $4,000 to $1,000 for those with incomes of $12,000 and over. A processing fee of $400 and plane fare of $400 are required for Korean adoptions, over and above the fee based on income. Out of area applicants also pay this cost for processing and transportation but if their study is done by another agency the fee based on income will differ. Indian placements include plane fare for parents and staff to and from Toronto. At the time of legal adoption of the child in all cases there is a court cost of $33.50, and legal fees of $100 for overseas adoption and $150 for U.S. adoption.

Adoption Procedures:

A couple writes for information about Welcome House, giving certain information about themselves. If the couple lives beyond the two-hundred-mile radius a local agency must be secured to study the family. Then they are invited to come together to a group meeting with other potential adoptive parents. After the homestudy is studied and approved for an out of area couple they may make formal application and then they are approved for placement. A study is done for area couples after application is approved. Pictures and information on a particular child are shared with a family and if the child is accepted the legal work begins.

Placement:

Families who are directly studied by Welcome House can consider the placement of Canadian Indian children over the age of six, as well as Korean children. Families for whom Welcome House does not do a study and is not directly responsible can only consider the full Korean and part-Korean child, but applicant cannot limit their consideration to a Korean Caucasian child only. Welcome House does not have available for placement the child under one year of age. Welcome House is unable to consider the placement of children from overseas with the single adoptive parent.

Approximate number of annual placements: 200-250.

World Vision International
919 West Huntington Drive
Monrovia, California 91016
(213) 357-1111

World Vision International is licensed by the government of Vietnam to process adoptions of Vietnamese children, and works through a licensed American adoption agency, Family Ministries, to make these placements. Family Ministries is licensed by the state of California.

Applicant Policies:

Placements are almost exclusively limited to residents of Los Angeles and Orange Counties in California. Applicants should be members of an evangelical Protestant Church, be married at least three years and be between 25-40 years of age when the family study begins.

Costs:

Total fees, payable to Family Ministries, would be $1700.

Adoption Procedure:

Families should contact Family Ministries, 6354 South Painter, Whittier, California 90601 telephone 213-698-9631 or 714-521-4343. This agency will do the homestudy and then process the applicants for a child selected. Most of the children are Vietnamese or Vietnamese-American children under school age, predominantly infants.

Approximate number of annual placements: 40.

At the time of printing the following group has closed applications because of long waiting lists:

Vietnam Orphanage Project
P.O. Box 35118
Ft. Louis, Washington

Licensure was pending from the state of Washington to place Vietnamese children from the Project's orphanages and polio center in Vietnam.

Bibliographies

Chapter References

This bibliography is arranged by chapters, with books and other reference material pertaining to each chapter listed by title and author. Each listing is described in detail in the Selected, Annotated Bibliography.

Introduction:

Berman, Claire. *We Take This Child: A Candid Look at Modern Adoption.*

Chapter One: The Decision to Adopt

Dywasuk, Colette T. *Adoption: Is It for You?*
Klibanoff, Elton and Susan. *Let's Talk About Adoption.*
Klein, Carole. *The Single Parent Experience.*
Marindin, Hope. *Handbook for Prospective Single Parents.*
Raymond, Louise. *Adoption and After* (revised by C. Dywasuk).

Chapter Two: Children for Adoption

Berman, Claire. *We Take This Child: A Candid Look at Modern Adoption.*
De Hartog. *The Children.*
International Adoption Handbook One. OURS.
International Adoption Handbook Two. OURS.
Rondell, Florence and Murray, Anne-Marie. *New Dimensions in Adoption.*

215

Bibliographies

On Older Children:

Jewett, Claudia L. *Adopting Older Children?*
McNamara, Joan. *Older Child Adoptions: An Overview.*
Nielson, Jacqueline. *Older Children Need Love Too.*
Pederson, Maia. *At Sixes and Sevens.*
Rose, Anna P. *Room for One More.*

On Transracial Adoptions:

Anderson, David. *Children of Special Value.*
Kramer, Betty. *The Unbroken Circle.*
Rigert, Joseph. *All Together.*
Salkmann, Victoria. *There Is a Child for You: A Family's Encounter with Modern Adoption.*

Chapter Three: Homestudies and Agencies

Berman, Claire. *We Take This Child: A Candid Look at Modern Adoption.*
Dywasuk, Colette. *Adoption: Is It for You?*
Klibanoff, Elton and Susan. *Let's Talk About Adoption.*
Salkmann, Victoria. *There Is a Child for You: A Family's Encounter with Modern Adoption.*

Chapter Four: Independent Adoptions

Berman, Claire. *We Take This Child.*
Chinnock, Frank. *Kim, A Gift from Vietnam.*
Klibanoff, Elton and Susan. *Let's Talk About Adoption.*

Chapter Five: Finding a Child

International Adoption Handbook Two. OURS.
Klibanoff, Elton and Susan. *Let's Talk About Adoption.*

Chapter Six: International Adoptions

Anderson, David. *Children of Special Value.*
Berman, Claire. *We Take This Child.*
Chinnock, Frank. *Kim, A Gift from Vietnam.*
De Hartog. *The Children.*
Kramer, Betty. *The Unbroken Circle.*
Margolies, Marjorie (title not yet released).
International Adoption Handbook One. OURS.
International Adoption Handbook Two. OURS.

Chapter Seven: Adoption Finances

AASK: Aid for the Adoption of Special Kids. AASK.

Bibliographies

Chapter Eight: Foster Care

Berman, Claire. *We Take This Child.*
Klibanoff, Elton and Susan. *Let's Talk About Adoption.*
Rose, Anna P. *Room for One More.*

Chapter Nine: Adoption and the Law

Goldstein, Joseph and Freud, Anna. *Beyond the Best Interests of the Child.*
Katz, Sanford N. *When Parents Fail: The Law's Response to Family Breakdown.*
Klibanoff, Elton and Susan. *Let's Talk About Adoption.*
Leavy, Martin L. *The Law of Adoption.*

Chapter Ten: Post Adoption

Anderson, David. *Children of Special Value.*
Berman, Claire. *We Take This Child.*
Fisher, Florence. *The Search for Anna Fisher.*
Jaffee, Benson and Fanshel, David. *How They Fared in Adoption: A Follow-up Study.*
Kadushin, Alfred. *Adopting Older Children.*
Kramer, Betty. *The Unbroken Circle.*
Jewett, Claudia. *Adopting Older Children?*
McNamara, Joan. *Older Child Adoptions: An Overview.*
Rigert, Joseph. *All Together.*
Rose, Anna P. *Room for One More.*
Triseliotis, John. *In Search of Origins: The Experiences of Adopted People.*
Rondell, Florence and Murray, Anne-Marie. *New Dimensions in Adoption.*

Family Reading

This bibliography has books recommended for family reading. Some books you will want to read with your children, others can be read by older children on their own. Descriptions of each book can be found in the Selected Annotated Bibliography.

Picture Books

Buck, Pearl. *Welcome Child.*
Caines, Jeanette. *Abby.*
Eisenberg, Eleanor. *The Pretty House That Found Happiness.*
McNamara, Joan. *The Ordinary Miracle.*
Meredith, Judy. *And Now We Are a Family.*
Partridge, Jackie. *My Journey Home.*
*Sheffield, Margaret. *Where Do Babies Come From?*

* This book is not concerned with adoption but with birth. However, it is one of the few books that deal with birth in such a way that adopted children can relate to the explanations without undue anxiety: it does not give value judgments to the relationships involved or project into the future.

Bibliographies

Taber, Barbara G. *Adopting Baby Brother.*
Waybill, Marjorie Ann. *Chinese Eyes.*

Books for Older Children

Buck, Pearl. *Matthew, Mark, Luke and John.*
Caudill, Rebecca. *Somebody Go and Bang a Drum.*
Doane, Pelagie. *Understanding Kim.*
Doss, Helen. *A Brother the Size of Me.*
————. *The Family That Nobody Wanted.*
————. *The Really Real Family.*
Johnson, Doris. *Su An.*
Murphy, Frances S. *A Ready-Made Family.*
Phroner, Mary. *Walk in My Mocassins.*

Selected, Annotated Bibliography

AASK: Aid for the Adoption of Special Kids. AASK, P.O. Box 11212, Oakland, Calif. 94611, 1975.

The AASK handbook was still in the planning stages at the time of this printing but was projected to cover such areas as state-by-state listing of specialized adoption programs, subsidies and medical programs; resources available on the local, state, and national level for the specialized needs of older, handicapped, and minority children; and personal narratives of families who have experienced the challenges and rewards of parenting "special" kids.

Anderson, David C. *Children of Special Value: Interracial Adoption in America.* New York: St. Martin's Press, 1971.

This excellent book is the work of a journalist who is also an adoptive parent. The first part explores the personal experiences of four families who adopted Korean, black, American Indian, and mixed-race children. The second part examines current adoption theories and some practical considerations in adoption across racial lines.

Berman, Claire. *We Take This Child: A Candid Look at Modern Adoption.* New York: Doubleday, 1974.

In this well-researched yet very human book, the author presents vivid pictures of the various diverse segments of today's adoption scene. Included in the personal adoption experiences that illustrate the main topics of the book is an adoption that failed.

Braithewaite, E. R. *Paid Servant.* New York: McGraw-Hill, 1968.

By the author of *To Sir, With Love,* this book brings across the difficulties of mixed-race children seeking adoptive homes. E. R. Braithwaite has writ-

218

ten this book based upon his own experiences in attempting to find a home for a particular child in London. It is at times bitter, at times hopeful, and most engrossing.

Buck, Pearl. *Children for Adoption*. New York: Random House, 1965.

Although the material in this book is now a bit dated, the plea for action on behalf of the countless children who wait for permanent loving homes is still just as strongly needed for the world community.

———. *Matthew, Luke, Mark, and John*. New York: John Day, 1964.

Through the story of one Korean boy, his friends, and their eventual adoption by American families, the difficult situation of some mixed-race children is described for readers in the nine-to-twelve age range.

———. *Welcome Child*. New York: Random House, 1964.

A picture book that uses photographs to illustrate the story of a Korean child's adoption by an American family, *Welcome Child* can be helpful to explain adoption to the youngest in the family.

Caines, Jeanette. *Abby*. New York: Harper and Row, 1973.

A joyous picture book about a little girl, who loves to hear the story of her arrival, written by Abby's mother.

Caudill, Rebecca. *Somebody Go and Bang a Drum*. New York: Dutton, 1974.

Aimed at the eight-to-twelve age group, the story tells of the growth of a family, from the birth of the first child to the adoption of the child who joins an interracial family of ten. It conveys the feelings of love and sharing that go into becoming part of a family "forever."

Children Who Wait: Proceedings of the Second International Conference on Interracial Adoption. Boston: The Open Door Society of Massachusetts, Inc., 1970.

The report of the highlights of the proceedings of the 1970 conference, including transcripts of some speeches and workshops.

Chinnock, Frank. *Kim: A Gift From Vietnam*. New York: World Publishers, 1969.

The story of a journalist's long struggle to adopt a Vietnamese orphan and her subsequent adjustment to life in an American family.

Connors, Grace. *Don't Disturb Daddy!* Boston: Brandon Press, 1965.

Told with a light, humorous touch, this is the story of the adoption of three older siblings, as written by their mother.

Bibliographies

De Hartog, Jan. *The Children: A Personal Record for the Use of Adoptive Parents.* New York: Antheneum, 1969.

A moving and practical book based on the adoption of two older Oriental children by the author. It is somewhat of a classic in the adoption field.

Doane, Pelagie. *Understanding Kim.* Philadelphia: Lippincott, 1962.

Children from nine to twelve can sympathize with the adjustments that must be made by both the biological children and the adopted child, in this case a new sister from Korea.

Doss, Helen. *A Brother the Size of Me.* Boston: Little, 1957.

The story of a boy whose family finally adopts a child just the right size. Treats adoption in a natural, matter-of-fact way, but emphasizes the enjoyment of a new arrival in the family.

————. *The Family Nobody Wanted.* Boston: Little, 1954.

Older children as well as adults can enjoy the story of the growth of an interracial family through adoption. Mrs. Doss conveys her common-sense attitudes about her own family in the 1950s.

————. *The Really Real Family.* Boston: Little, 1959.

The story of the adoption of two sisters into the Doss family, who at last have a "really real family."

Dywasuk, Collette Taube. *Adoption: Is It for You?* New York: Harper and Row, 1973.

A general overview of adoption with helpful information about evaluating yourself and adoption possibilities. It is somewhat lacking, however, in accurate information concerning international adoptions, and information on adoption of infants is now dated, even two years later.

Eisenberg, Eleanor. *The Pretty House That Found Happiness.* Austin, Texas: Steck-Vaughn Co., 1964.

A picture book about a man and woman and their home, who were all very lonely until a child came to stay through adoption, making a "stay-together-forever-family." Because it does not concentrate on "choosing a special baby," this book can be appropriate for some children adopted after infancy.

Fanshel, David. *Far From the Reservation: The Transracial Adoption of American Indian Children.* Metuchen, New Jersey: Scarecrow, 1972.

The author examines and interprets the results of the Indian Adoption Research Project of 1964, discussing how the adoption of American Indian children into white homes has affected the children, their adoptive families, and the future of the tribal system.

Bibliographies

Fanshel, David, and Eugene B. Shinn. *Dollars and Sense in Foster Care of Children: A Look at Cost Factors.* New York: Child Welfare League of America, 1972.

This book has had a significant impact on many parts of the foster care system, not the least of which is the legislature. By showing in hard, logical detail how the systems that trap children also trap the taxpayer with significantly higher cost outlay, the authors have hit the public in the pocketbook.

Fisher, Florence. *The Search for Anna Fisher.* New York: Arthur Fields-Dutton, 1973.

Florence Fisher is a founder of ALMA, the Adoptees Liberty Movement Associates, which advocates the removal of barriers—legal, social, and agency—that prevent adopted adults from discovering their biological heritages. This is her personal story of the search for Anna Fisher, the biological mother who gave her up for adoption as an infant.

Fourth Annual Conference on Adoptable Children. Washington, D.C.: D.C. Metropolitan Area Council on Adoptable Children, 1974.

The Conference proceedings are outlined in great detail including voluminous preconference research reports, task force papers, and speech and workshop transcripts.

Frontiers in Adoption. Ann Arbor, Mich.: Council on Adoptable Children, 1967.

The report of a 1967 conference on new aspects of adoption such as placement of minority and older children, with reports, papers, and conference results.

Goldstein, Joseph; Anna Freud; and Albert Solnit. *Beyond the Best Interests of the Child.* New York: The Free Press-Macmillan, 1973.

Almost from the moment of its publication, this book began to have far-reaching and significant effects on decisions affecting children in divorce, adoption, and foster care. It is a must for anyone concerned with the welfare of children and should be required reading for every judge and legislator.

Haitch, Richard. *Orphans of the Living: The Foster Care Crisis.* New York: Public Affairs Committee in cooperation with the Child Welfare League of America, 1968.

This book explores the dilemma of the foster care system and recommends action.

Harrison-Ross, Phyllis, and Barbara Wyden. *The Black Child: A Parent's Guide.* New York: Wyden, 1973.

This book is not directly concerned with adoption, but can be of help to white families who have adopted across racial lines. The book is primarily directed at black parents of black children, but the insights can be valuable for all parents.

Haywood, Carolyn. *Here's Penny*. New York: Harcourt, 1965.

One of a series of children's books by the author for the child who can read on his own, the book discusses the adoption of an older child in a matter-of-fact way as part of the larger plot.

Herzog, Elizabeth, *et al. Families for Black Children: The Search for Adoptive Parents*. Parts I and II. Children's Bureau, Office of Child Development, U.S. Department of Health, Education and Welfare in co-operation with the Social Research Group, George Washington University. Washington, D.C.: U.S. Government Printing Office, 1971.

This report discusses the possibilities for adoption of black children, exploring traditional approaches and drawing conclusions for the future.

Holt, Bertha (Mrs. Harry). *Seed from the East*. New York: Oxford Press, 1956.

The story of the adoption of the first mixed-race Korean children by Harry Holt and the religious convictions that strengthened him in his struggle. It is written by his wife, who remains active in the adoption work of what is now Holt Children's Services, one of the largest adoption agencies in the world.

International Adoption Handbook One. Minneapolis, Minn.: OURS (Organization for a United Response), 1972.

This excellent handbook is published by an adoptive parents group with considerable experience in international adoption, particularly with so-called "hard-to-place" children. The book focuses primarily on Korea—bibliographies, recipes, vocabulary lists, medical information, personal narratives—but parents of other adopted children may well find much of it insightful. Cost is $2.00 plus postage for each Handbook, One and Two.

International Adoption Handbook Two. Minneapolis, Minn.: OURS, 1973.

This second handbook gives more information on Korea plus specific Vietnamese and Colombian sections. There is also a good deal more general information concerning naturalization, adoption procedures, English as a second language, and the adoption of older children. It can be useful for parents whose adopted children are from a foreign country, and also those who adopted their children in the United States.

Jaffee, Benson, and David Fanshel. *How They Fared in Adoption: A Follow-up Study*. New York and London: Columbia University Press, 1970.

The findings of a research study sponsored by the Child Welfare League of America discusses the life adjustments of a hundred adults who were adopted as children.

Bibliographies

Jewitt, Claudia L. *Adopting Older Children?* Boston: The Northeast Adoption Council, c/o Massachusetts Open Door Society, 1973. Cost is $2.00 plus postage.

This is the most useful and insightful book on the adoption of older children now published. In barely thirty pages it covers all aspects and problems with sensitivity and common sense, based on the practical considerations of actual parents and social workers involved with adoptions of older children. There is no table of contents but there is an index tracing stages in adopting an older child. Most highly recommended.

Johnson, Doris. *Su An*. Chicago: Follett, 1968.

The delicate line drawings by artist Leonard Weisgard harmonize with the fragile text telling the story of a little girl who leaves Korea and memories of her biological mother to go to the United States for adoption by an American family. It is a sensitive and moving book, meant to be read aloud to your children at a quiet time.

Kadushin, Alfred. *Adopting Older Children*. New York: Columbia University Press, 1970.

The results of a follow-up study on a number of children adopted out of infancy and the adjustments they made in their families.

Kirk, H. David. *Shared Fate: A Theory of Adoption and Mental Health*. New York: The Free Press of Glencoe, 1964.

An adoptive parent who is also a mental health professional discusses his theories based on studies and observations of relationships between adoptive parents and their children.

Klein, Carole. *The Single Parent Experience*. New York: Walker, 1973.

This book discusses all aspects about the single person who is a parent or wishes to become one. One section deals specifically with adoption and the considerations that should be made by a single person contemplating adoption.

Klibanoff, Elton and Susan. *Let's Talk About Adoption*. Boston: Little, Brown, 1973.

This book discusses the adoption process and the current adoption scene in clear language. It is most useful to parents considering adoption for their families. Also included are model reform laws and background on legal and historical aspects of modern adoption.

Leavy, Martin L. *Law of Adoption*. Dobbs Ferry, N.Y.: Oceana, 1968.

A handbook of legal aspects of adoption, still useful even though much of the information is dated and has been superseded.

223

Bibliographies

Margolies, Marjorie. (Title to be announced.)

This book was in the planning stages at the time of this printing, with publication projected for late 1975. It will be an account of the experiences of Ms. Margolies, an NBC reporter and single adoptive parent, as she planned the adoption of her Korean and Vietnamese daughters. Ms. Margolies's firsthand accounts of the situations in Korea and Vietnam and the needs of children will be a major part of the book.

Marindin, Hope. *Handbook for Prospective Single Parents.* Washington, D.C.: Single Parents Committee of Metropolitan Washington, c/o Council on Adoptable Children (COAC) of Metropolitan Washington.

This is a twenty-five-page handbook of information for the benefit of single persons who have decided to adopt. It contains specific data on sources for single parent adoptions, costs, legal provisions, changes in lifestyle, and other areas. Cost is $1.25 (including postage) and orders should go to 3824 Legation Street N.W., Washington, D.C. 20015.

McNamara, Joan. *Older Child Adoptions: An Overview.* Dobbs Ferry, N.Y.: AFW (Adoptive Families of Westchester), 1975.

A wide-ranging handbook covering recruitment, education, and support in the adoption of the school aged child. It includes a section with personal stories by adoptive parents and by adopted children. Cost $3.75.

McNamara, Joan. *The Ordinary Miracle.* Dobbs Ferry, N.Y.: AFW, 1975.

Two children's stories make up this book: one on what families are like, with many different families sharing together, and the second the story of how a child came to be adopted into a family. The adoption story is written so that it can be used with almost any adopted child, whatever age, race, sex, or nationality. Cost $1.75 plus $.25 postage.

McWhinnie, Alexina. *Adopted Children: How They Grow Up.* Atlantic Highlands, N.J.: Humanities, 1967.

A study of adults adopted as children and the affect that adoption has had upon their lives.

Meredith, Judy. *And Now We Are a Family.* Boston: Beacon Press, 1972.

A gentle picture book with simple crayonlike drawings that look as though a child had done them, this book talks of how a child becomes part of a family forever after adoption. The mention of unwed mothers may make this otherwise commendable book inappropriate for some adoption situations.

Mixed Race Adoptions. Quebec, Canada: Open Door Society, 1970.

This is the report of the first international conference on mixed-race adoptions, held in Canada in 1969, with transcripts of the major speeches and workshops.

Bibliographies

Murphy, Frances Salomon. *Ready-Made Family*. New York: Scholastic Book Service, 1972.

The story of three school-age siblings placed in a new home, written for the nine-to-twelve age range. It talks of the adjustments that have to be made, and the thoughts and feelings of the children.

Nielsen, Jacqueline. *Older Children Need Love Too*. Washington, D.C.: Children's Bureau, U.S. Department of Health, Education and Welfare, 1973.

This is the description of a special adoption program in San Diego for older children. It explores the child's psychological difficulties in a way that makes it useful to parents in understanding their child's emotional needs. Cost is $.40, and orders should go the U.S. Government Printing Office, Washington, D.C. 20402. The pamphlet is DHEW Publication Number OCD 73-16.

Neufield, John. *Edgar Allen*. New York: Signet, 1969.

This adult novel focuses on the failure of an interracial adoption, written from the perspective of the twelve-year-old son in the family.

Palmer, Frances. *And Four to Grow On*. New York: Rinehart, 1960.

A mother's story of the family's adoption of two sets of school-age siblings.

Partridge, Jackie. *My Journey Home*. Minneapolis, Minn.: OURS, 1974.

A unique book that tells the story of how and why a child is adopted from Korea. It is a simple, clear text with pictures and places to add your own child's drawings and photographs. At the back is a page to record immunizations, height, and weight. This is the only published book available that can be used to tell your child's own special adoption story in a simple way without your putting together a book on your own. Available from OURS for $2.00. A Vietnam adaptation will be published soon.

Paton, Jean. *Orphan Voyage*. New York: Vantage, 1968.

A book written to describe the search for the past by adopted adults by the founder of Orphan Voyage, a program of mutual aid and guidance for adults searching for parents or relatives, located in Cedar Edge, Colorado.

Pederson, Mai. *At Sixes and Sevens*. Cleveland: World, 1969.

The insightful narrative of the adoption of two school-aged sisters, told by their adoptive mother.

Phroner, Mary. *Walk in My Moccasins*. Philadelphia: Westminster, 1966.

The story of the adoption of five Sioux Indian siblings.

Bibliographies

Raymond, Louise. *Adoption and After*. Rev. ed. by Colette T. Dywasuk. New York: Harper and Row, 1974.

The dated information in this book has been revised by Mrs. Dywasuk, author of *Adoption: Is It for You?* so that factual information is even more current than in Mrs. Dywasuk's own book. The text is psychologically oriented and can provide insights into your own feelings and considerations in adoption.

Rigert, Joseph. *All Together*. New York: Harper and Row, 1974.

A particularly enjoyable book about a particularly enjoyable family, the Rigerts of Minneapolis. Although an interracial adoptive family of eight children and two parents and assorted pets can't really be called typical, it is the average day-to-day occurrences that point out how this family, like other families, grows through problems, challenges, and daily sharing. It is an important book for those considering adoption across racial lines and those who have already adopted children, and enjoyable for those who just want to know what it's all about.

————. *Europe on Eight Kids a Day*. Minneapolis, Minn.: Dillon Press, 1971.

A father's account of travels across Europe with his interracial family.

Rondell, Florence R. and Murray, Anne-Marie. *New Dimensions in Adoption*. New York: Crown Publishers, 1974.

This excellent new book is addressed to those interested in the adoption of a waiting child, the older, handicapped or minority child in need of adoption. The special needs of such children and the range of appropriate and helpful responsive ways these can be dealt with are a major part of this book, within the framework of basic approaches in family life. This book is highly recommended to those people considering the adoption of a special child, as well as to professionals.

————. *Room for One More*. New York: Houghton, 1950.

This book is now very old but the insights contained in its pages are still as fresh as ever. Mrs. Rose writes of her experiences raising older foster children with love and common sense.

Salkman, Victoria. *There Is a Child for You: A Family's Encounter with Modern Adoption*. New York: Simon and Schuster, 1973.

This is the personal account of one family's experiences as they attempt to adopt a child of minority background. It will be familiar to those who have already adopted and provides private glimpses into the adoption process for those who have not.

Bibliographies

Sheffield, Margaret. *Where Do Babies Come From?* New York: Alfred A. Knopf, 1974.

This picture book is based on an award-winning BBC program now used with children through the English schools. It does not mention adoption but may be one of the few books on birth that can be used with adoptive children without raising undue anxiety over values or relationships.

Taber, Barbara G. *Adopting Baby Brother*. Rochester, N.Y.: P.O. Box 5061, River Station, Rochester, N.Y. 14627, 1974.

This privately printed book is a delight to read, relating the adoption of a baby boy into a family with two girls. The theme of interracial adoption is gently explored through the text and lovely color pictures. The cost is $2.50 plus 25 cents postage.

Thesis Book. Minneapolis, Minn.: OURS, 1973.

A collection of theses, studies, and reports on the adjustment, problems, and outcomes of adoptions in Minnesota. Most of the studies deal with adoptions across racial lines, primarily of Korean children. Cost is $4.00.

Thompson, Jean. *The House of Tomorrow*. New York: Harper and Row, 1967.

The experiences of an unwed mother, written in diary form by a woman who struggled to deal with her situation independently. It is a picture on the other side of the closed curtain of adoption, one seldom seem.

Triseliotis, John. *In Search of Origins: The Experiences of Adopted People*. Boston and New York: Routlege and Kegan Paul, 1973.

This is the most recent book on what happens after adoption, from the viewpoint of adults now looking for their biological roots.

Waybill, Marjorie Ann. *Chinese Eyes*. Scottsdale, Pa.: Herald Press, 1974.

This children's book is written by an adoptive parent about her daughter's personal experience with the realities of being "different."

Index

Index

Index

Index